THE CATHOLIC UNIVERSITY OF AMERICA
CANON LAW STUDIES
No. 331

# THE CONSTITUTION AND SUPREME ADMINISTRATION OF REGIONAL SEMINARIES SUBJECT TO THE SACRED CONGREGATION FOR THE PROPAGATION OF THE FAITH IN CHINA

## A HISTORICAL SYNOPSIS AND A COMMENTARY

*by the*

REVEREND MARCIAN J. MATHIS, O.F.M., J.C.L.
Priest of the St. Louis Province of the
Most Sacred Heart of Jesus

A DISSERTATION

*Submitted to the Faculty of the School of Canon Law of the Catholic University of America in Partial Fulfillment of the Requirements for the Degree of Doctor of Canon Law*

THE CATHOLIC UNIVERSITY OF AMERICA PRESS
WASHINGTON, D. C.
1952

NIHIL OBSTAT:
Eduardus G. Roelker, S. T. D., J. C. D.
*Censor Deputatus*
Washingtonii, D. C., die 20 Maii, 1952.

IMPRIMI POTEST:
Eligius Weir, O. F. M.
*Minister Provincialis*
Sancti Ludovici, Mo., die 23 Maii, 1952.

NIHIL OBSTAT:
Pancratius Freudinger, O. F. M., L. G.
*Censor Deputatus*
Teutopoli, Ill., die 3 Iulii, 1952.

IMPRIMATUR:
✠ Gulielmus A. O'Connor, D. D.
*Episcopus Campifontis-in-Illinois*
Campifonte-in-Illinois, die 5 Iulii, 1952.



*Printed by The Abbey Press, St. Meinrad, Indiana*

DEDICATED
TO
THE CHRISTIANS
OF
CHINA

# TABLE OF CONTENTS

Page
FOREWORD .......... ix

## Part I

HISTORICAL SYNOPSIS

CHAPTER

I. THE TRIDENTINE SEMINARY .......... 1

II. HISTORICAL DEVELOPMENT OF THE LAW ON THE CONSTITUTION AND ADMINISTRATION OF REGIONAL SEMINARIES IN CHINA .......... 8
Article 1. From the Council of Trent to 1845 .......... 8
Article 2. From 1845 to the Code of Canon Law .......... 13
Article 3. The First Plenary Council of China .......... 18

III. ACTUAL ESTABLISHMENT OF REGIONAL SEMINARIES IN CHINA .......... 24
Article 1. The Movement toward Regional Seminaries .. 24
Article 2. The Regulations of 1921 and 1934 .......... 32
Article 3. Constitution of 15 Regional Seminaries Subject to the Sacred Congregation for the Propagation of the Faith .......... 39
1. Regional Seminary of Sui-yüan .......... 39
2. Regional Seminary of Hsin-ching (Hsinking) ...... 41
3. Regional Seminary of Süan-hua .......... 42
4. Regional Seminary of Cha-la .......... 43
5. Regional Seminary of Ching-hsien (Kinghsien) ... 44
6. Regional Seminary of Chi-nan (Tsinan) .......... 45
7. Regional Seminary of Ta-t'ung .......... 46
8. Regional Seminary of T'ai-yüan .......... 48
9. Regional Seminary of Lan-chou (Lanchow) ....... 49
10. Regional Seminary of Shang-hai .......... 50
11. Regional Seminary of Wu-hu .......... 51
12. Regional Seminary of K'ai-feng .......... 52
13. Regional Seminary of Han-k'ou (Hankow) ........ 52
14. Regional Seminary of Fu-chien (Fukien) ......... 54
15. Regional Seminary of Hsiang-kang (Hongkong) ... 55
Appendix. Intermissional Seminaries .......... 58
1. Intermissional Seminary of Yen-chou (Yenchow) .. 59
2. Intermissional Seminary of Ning-po .......... 59
3. Intermissional Seminary of Ch'eng-tu .......... 60

## Part II

### CANONICAL COMMENTARY

CHAPTER — Page

IV. FUNDAMENTAL LAW OF THE CODE OF CANON LAW ... 61
- Article 1. Distinction of Various Types of Seminaries .. 61
- Article 2. Authority Required to Establish a Regional Seminary ... 63
- Article 3. Application of the Law in Mission Lands .... 68
- Article 4. The Constitution of Regional Seminaries Subject to the Sacred Congregation for the Propagation of the Faith ... 71

V. THE SUPREME DIRECTION OF REGIONAL SEMINARIES ... 74
- Article 1. The Rights of the Sacred Congregation for the Propagation of the Faith ... 76
- Article 2. Attendance at the Regional Seminary ... 80
- Article 3. Prohibition against Entrance into a Religious Institute ... 84
- Article 4. Differences in the *Norme* of 1921 ... 89

VI. RIGHTS AND DUTIES OF THE SUPERIOR GENERAL OF THE INSTITUTE ... 92
- Article 1. Appointment of Officials and Professors ..... 92
- Article 2. Rules of Discipline and Program of Studies .. 97
- Article 3. The Agreement for the Economic Administration of the Regional Seminary ... 106

VII. RIGHTS AND DUTIES OF THE ORDINARIES OF THE REGION ... 110
- Article 1. The Ordinary and His Students ... 111
- Article 2. The Ordinaries and the Administration of the Seminary ... 124
- Article 3. Differences in the *Norme* of 1921 ... 131

VIII. RIGHTS AND DUTIES OF THE RECTOR ... 134
- Article 1. The Office of Rector ... 134
- Article 2. Exemption of the Seminary from the Jurisdiction of the Local Pastor ... 138
- Article 3. Differences in the *Norme* of 1921 ... 146

## Part III

### DOCUMENTS

Page

Document 1. Note Relative à un Séminaire Régional pour la Chine du Centre et du Nord ..................... 148

Document 2. Projet d'Organisation et d'Administration du Séminaire Central de Tatung ..................... 149

Document 3. Norme per i Seminari Regionali in Cina ........ 151

Document 4. Conventio Ordinariorum pro Seminario Regionali de Hongkong ..................... 154

Document 5. Conventio ... inter Ordinarios Regionis Eccl. de Fukien et Ordinem Praedicatorum .............. 155

CONCLUSIONS ..................... 157

BIBLIOGRAPHY ..................... 159

ABBREVIATIONS ..................... 163

INDEX OF PLACES NAMES

I. Wade-Giles Transliteration ..................... 164

II. Postal Guide Transliteration ..................... 166

ALPHABETICAL INDEX ..................... 168

BIOGRAPHICAL NOTE ..................... 173

MAP OF CHINA SHOWING LOCATION OF THE REGIONAL SEMINARIES ..................... 174

CANON LAW STUDIES ..................... 176

# FOREWORD

The field of missionary law is as yet comparatively undeveloped and largely even unexplored. A case in point is the regional major seminary for the training of the native clergy, an institution which until recently had received but meager attention in books of missionary law. The present work proposes to study this institution through the official acts of the Popes, of the Sacred Congregations, and of the mission superiors, and to point out the practical application of these acts to and in China. The work purports, therefore, to explain the organization and administration of this providential instrument for the development and consolidation of the Church in China and in other mission lands.

With China gone communist, this study may seem out of step and futile. But it looks to the future and hopes to help keep aglow the spark of missionary zeal and initiative that may re-enkindle the fire of Christianity in China once the Communist persecution has been overcome. The blood of Christians is seed also in China, where the Church has suffered long periods of persecution and proscription before, notably during the Ming (1368-1644) and the Ch'ing (1644-1912) dynasties, and emerged the stronger for them. It is also hoped that other mission territories will profit by the review of, and commentary on, the legislation for the foundation and direction of regional seminaries in China.

This study is divided into three parts. Part I outlines the historical setting. It surveys the legislation from the Council of Trent to the promulgation of the Code of Canon Law; it relates the main events leading to the establishment of regional seminaries in China; and it presents a brief account of each of the fifteen regional seminaries founded in China by the Sacred Congregation for the Propagation of the Faith. Part II offers a canonical commentary on the individual provisions of the special regulations drawn up by the Sacred Congregation for the Propagation of the Faith for the constitution and government of regional seminaries in mission lands. Part III publishes for the first time a number of important documents bearing on the foundation and the administration of such seminaries.

As a matter of style, Chinese toponyms are transliterated according to the Wade and Giles system as used in *Gazetteer of Chinese Place Names, Based on the Index to V. K. Ting Atlas, Compiled by the United States Board on Geographical Names* (Washington, D.C.: Army Map Service, 1944). For the convenience of those who are not familiar with this system, the toponyms are transliterated in parentheses according to the system usually employed in mission publications.

A debt of gratitude is acknowledged to the Very Reverend Eligius Weir, O.F.M., Provincial Superior of the Franciscan Province of the Most Sacred Heart, St. Louis, Mo., for granting the writer the opportunity of advanced study in Canon Law; to the Faculty of the School of Canon Law, Catholic University of America, Washington, D.C., for kindly interest and scholarly guidance; to the Right Reverend Monsignor Adamo Pucci of the Sacred Congregation for the Propagation of the Faith, Rome, for his tireless efforts in securing and annotating the documents which have made this study possible; to the Reverend Dr. Antonio Sisto Rosso, O.F.M., Franciscan Monastery, Washington, D.C., for his advice and expert assistance in the field of Sinology, particularly in problems of Chinese toponymy; and to all others who have helped to bring this work to a successful conclusion.

# PART I
# HISTORICAL SYNOPSIS

## CHAPTER I
## THE TRIDENTINE SEMINARY

The twenty-third session of the Council of Trent convened on July 15, 1563. In this session, chapter 18 of the decrees on reform concerns seminaries. It is entitled: "Directions for establishing seminaries for clerics, especially the younger ones; in their erection many things are to be observed; the education of those to be promoted to cathedral and major churches."[1] The gist of this legislation is as follows:

1. The holy council decrees that all cathedral and metropolitan churches, and churches greater than these, shall be bound to provide for the education and training in ecclesiastical discipline of a certain number of boys of their city or diocese or province, in a college near the said churches or in some other suitable place chosen by the bishop.

2. The boys must be at least 12 years of age. They must be of legitimate birth and inclined to the priesthood. The sons of the poor are preferred, but the rich are not excluded, provided they pay their expenses and are otherwise fit for the seminary and the ministry.

3. The Bishop shall divide the boys into as many classes as he deems proper, according to their age and progress in discipline, and when opportune shall assign some to the ministry. Others he shall keep in the college to be further educated and he shall replace by still others those who have been withdrawn, so that the college may be a perpetual seminary of ecclesiastical vocations.

[1] *Concilii Tridentini Diariorum, Actorum, Epistolarum, Tractatuum, Nova Collectio.* Edidit Societas Goerresiana (13 vols., Friburgi Brisgoviae: Herder, 1901-), IX, 628-630 (hereafter cited *Nova Collectio Soc. Goerr.*).

4. The students shall study grammar, singing, ecclesiastical computation, and other useful arts; they shall be instructed in Sacred Scripture, ecclesiastical books, the homilies of the saints, the manner of administering the sacraments, especially of hearing confessions, and the rites and ceremonies of the Church.

5. They shall wear the clerical tonsure and garb. They shall attend daily mass, confess once a month, and receive Holy Communion in accordance with the directions of their confessor. On feast days they shall serve in the cathedral and other churches of the locality.

6. All these things, and others beneficial and needful, the Bishop shall prescribe with the advice of two of the senior canons chosen by himself. These same shall visit the seminary often.

7. The greater part of the decree deals with the practical problem of financing the new institute. A board of administration is to be set up, consisting of the Bishop, two canons of the chapter, and two of the city clergy. Since for the construction of the college, the paying of the teachers and servants, the maintenance of the youths and other expenses, revenues are necessary, the Bishop and the board are empowered to tax the chapter, all dignities, offices, prebends, colleges, benefices, churches, associations, and monasteries of whatever kind and rank. Three classes of institutions are exempt: the colleges which are themselves seminaries; the monasteries of Mendicants, and the tithes belonging to the brethren of St. John of Jerusalem.

8. The professors and their manner of teaching are wholly dependent on the judgment of the Bishop. In the future the professorships shall not be conferred on any but doctors or masters and licentiates of Sacred Scripture or Canon Law, or on other competent persons who can personally discharge that office.

9. Regional seminaries: if in any province the dioceses are too poor to have a college, the provincial synod or the metropolitan with two of the oldest suffragans shall estab-

lish one or more colleges at the metropolitan or other church of the province, where the youths of the province may be educated.

10. In churches having extensive dioceses, the Bishop may have one or more colleges in the diocese as he may deem expedient; which however shall in all things be dependent on the one erected and established in the metropolitan city.

11. This decree is a general norm, the Bishop is to apply it to the needs of his diocese. If any difficulty should arise by reason of which the establishment or maintenance of the seminary is hindered or disrupted, the Bishop and his directors or the provincial synod shall have the authority to decide and regulate all matters necessary or expedient for the happy advancement of the seminary, even to modify or augment, if need be, the contents of this decree.[2]

From these regulations and from their interpretation by the Bishops of the late sixteenth century it is evident that the Tridentine seminary was an institution which completely reorganized the training of the clergy. The students live a common life and are shut off from communication with the outer world. The students are given their instruction within the seminary. It is not in accord with the decree of the Council of Trent that the clerics study in institutions which are not connected immediately with the seminary. Nor is it consonant with the Council of Trent that other students not called to the priesthood be taken into this institution, much less that those who are called to some other vocation in life be educated there.[3] Furthermore, the new school is absolutely dependent on the Ordinary of the diocese. Finally, all available funds are to be turned to the providing of good professors and the education of the poor students free of charge.

[2] *Nova Collectio Soc. Goerr.*, IX, 628-630. The entire decree may also be found in the handy little volume: *Canons and Decrees of the Council of Trent*, ed. H. Schroeder, O.P. (St. Louis, Mo.: Herder, 1941). Latin text: pp. 446-450. English translation: pp. 175-179.

[3] P. Hinschius, *System des katholischen Kirchenrechts* (4 vols., Berlin: Verlag von I. Guttentag, 1869-1888), IV, 504.

### *Further Development*

The reform of clerical education had been achieved in as far as there was discovered the institution that was best suited to prepare and educate a learned clergy. The legislation on seminaries from the time of the Council of Trent to the present was based on this decree of the council. But the legislation of the council was general—it was left to the Bishops to apply it to the particular needs of their dioceses. That this was indeed done by the Bishops is evident from the decrees of particular councils held after the Council of Trent, for they are replete with seminary legislation. St. Charles Borromeo was foremost in this respect. His activities give us the full picture of the new institute envisioned by the Council of Trent. The zealous reformer had a seminary opened in Milan even before he took up residence there. The first Milanese seminary was opened by Monsignor Ormaneto, Borromeo's Vicar General, on the 10th of December, 1564.[4] This seminary developed into the major theological seminary of Milan and in 1572 had already 140 clerical students with 15 professors.

St. Charles also developed the Tridentine ideal of a plurality of seminaries for larger dioceses. He proceeded to institute seminaries which were fitted to the various ages and talents of the students—a division which has been kept ever since. Thus St. Charles considered it necessary to found a secondary seminary called the "della Canonica." The clerics here studied only moral theology, since they were not fit for deeper study. St. Charles also founded several rural seminaries for the special purpose of furnishing priests for the mountain districts. The candidates for these seminaries were chosen from the mountain places, with the consequent assurance of a more effective apostolate in these regions.[5]

[4] C. Orsenigo, *Life of St. Charles Borromeo* (St. Louis, Mo.: Herder, 1945), pp. 47-80.

[5] Orsenigo, *Life of St. Charles Borromeo*, pp. 80-81.

### *St. Charles' Legislation*

If St. Charles was active in actually establishing seminaries, he was not less zealous in backing up his activities with proper legislation. A month after he entered Milan, Borromeo called his first provincial council and proclaimed the reform of the Council of Trent, also decreeing the many particulars necessary for its complete observance. During his 20 years of residence, Borromeo held six provincial councils and eleven diocesan synods, the acts of which are all very well preserved and handed down to us in the second volume of the *Acta Ecclesiae Mediolanensis.* Most of these councils put special emphasis on the seminary legislation of the Council of Trent. Thus they give particular instructions on the funds to be collected, the visitation of the Bishop, the studies, the spiritual and temporal administration, etc.[6]

But St. Charles Borromeo's complete and perfected plan of what the Tridentine seminary should be is contained in his famous *Institutiones.* This legislation of the Cardinal is the perfect complement of the decree of the Council of Trent, because in it we find the details of that institution which the Fathers of the council envisioned in a more general way. Since the Council of Trent left it to the Bishops to draw up a rule of life and administration for the seminary, Borromeo decreed that these *Institutiones* be observed in all the seminaries within and outside the city.[7]

*The first part* contains particulars relating to the administration of the seminary. Its ten chapters concern:

The spiritual government, mentioning such things as retreats, divine office, ceremonies, holy orders, etc.

Studies—exact rules on various classes in grammar, in the humanities, rhetoric, philosophy, theology, sacred scripture, and cases of conscience. Text books are prescribed and

[6] *Acta Ecclesiae Mediolanensis,* edited by Achille Ratti and Raphael Ferraris (4 vols., Milan: Pontifical Press of St. Joseph, 1890-1892), II, 56-58, 252-253, 632-635 (hereafter cited *Acta Eccl. Med.*).

[7] The complete text of the *Institutiones* can be found in the *Acta Eccl. Med.,* III, 95-146.

the time spent on each subject is determined. Pastoral theology is to be taught immediately before ordination. Classes in sacred eloquence and chant are prescribed.

Finances—rules on the common table, reports of funds to the Ordinary, the books of administration, the treasury.

Daily *horarium*—this differed according to the seasons of the year. Exact prescriptions from rising to bed time.

Vacations and recreation—pastors must watch over the students. Formula of the letter sent to each pastor giving instructions on what is expected of the seminarian during vacation.

Visitation—the Bishop shall visit the seminary at least once every year etc.

Candidates—detailed rules on admittance, examinations to be made, investigations, necessary articles to be brought by the boys.[8]

*The second part* concerns the officials of the seminary, and in ten chapters gives detailed instructions on the various duties of the rector, vice-rector, confessors, prefect of studies, teachers and professors, procurator, prefects of discipline, librarians, and finally also the servants.[9]

*The third part,* in seven chapters, concerns the daily life of the student. The purpose of the seminary is clearly set forth, exercises of piety and liturgical functions are prescribed. Then follow rules of discipline, the manner of studying, the wearing of the clerical garb, the manner of performing the domestic labor such as making one's bed and sweeping the room, and the manner in which one ought to act when outside the seminary. The last chapter deals with the care of the sick.[10]

### *Résume*

This summary account of the activities, of the legislation and of the *Institutiones* of St. Charles Borromeo serves to reflect the ideal of the Tridentine seminary. The *Institu-*

[8] *Acta Eccl. Med.,* III, 95-116.
[9] *Acta Eccl. Med.,* III, 119-135.
[10] *Acta Eccl. Med.,* III, 135-146.

*tiones* of St. Charles have served as the best guide for all succeeding Bishops and have given us the complete picture of just what the Tridentine seminary was to be. Clerical education had gone through a dark period during the three centuries immediately preceding the Council of Trent. But now the institution of clerical training best suited for the needs of the Church had been found. Pallavicino (1607-1667) stated that many of the Fathers of the Council at the close of the twenty-third session expressed their belief that, if nothing else had been accomplished, yet the fact of the new seminary legislation had amply rewarded them for all the work they had done.[11]

[11] S. Pallavicino, *Istoria del Concilio di Trento* (3 vols., Naples, 1757), XXI, c. 8, n. 3.

## CHAPTER II

## HISTORICAL DEVELOPMENT OF THE LAW ON THE CONSTITUTION AND THE ADMINISTRATION OF REGIONAL SEMINARIES IN CHINA

### ARTICLE 1. FROM THE COUNCIL OF TRENT TO 1845

The basic legislation for the constitution and administration of seminaries in China is the decree of the 18th chapter of the 23rd session *de reformatione* of the Council of Trent. The legislation of the council has been reported in detail in chapter one of this dissertation. Of special importance for China is the provision made by the Fathers of the council that, if any difficulty should arise by reason of which the establishment or maintenance of the seminary might be hindered, the Bishop with his board, or the provincial synod, should have the authority to decide and regulate all matters which appeared necessary and expedient for the happy advancement of the seminary, and if need be even to modify or augment the contents of the council's decree.

The decree of the ecumenical council was not meant for Europe only, but for the whole Church. All dioceses were to strive to have a seminary for the education of the future clergy. The Sacred Congregation of Propaganda was not slow to remind the mission superiors that this duty belonged to them also. The documents quoted in this work refer to China only, either directly in that they were addressed to the Vicars Apostolic in China, or indirectly in so far as they were meant for superiors of missions who had regional seminaries in which also students were trained for the Chinese missions.

The instructions, decrees, letters and so forth, of the period under consideration deal primarily with the duty of the Vicars Apostolic to establish seminaries. Let us point out the more important of these documents. First of all an instruction to the first Vicars Apostolic, in 1659, reminded the new Vicars setting out for the kingdoms of China, Tonkin and Cochin-China, that the principal reason for sending Bishops into these regions is that they attend by all means to train a native clergy and thus provide for those vast regions committed to their care.[1] The constitution of Alexander VII, *Sacrosancti Apostolatus officii,* 18 Jan. 1658,[2] the Constitution of the same Pontiff, *Super cathedram,* 9 Sept. 1659,[3] and the Constitutions of Clement IX, both of 13 Sept. 1669, namely *Speculatores* and *In excelsa,*[4] as well as that of Clement X, *Decet Romanum Pontificem,* 23 Dec. 1673[5]—all spoke in the same manner, that the principal end in view in the sending of these episcopal Vicars to China, Tonkin, Cochin-China, Siam and other neighboring kingdoms, was that clerics and priests be formed from the ranks of the native Christians, and that the gradual growth of the Faith and the increase in the number of Christians should gradually introduce the observance of the ecclesiastical discipline. And in the same manner did many other decrees and constitutions provide, especially the Brief of Innocent XI, *Onerosa pastoralis,* 1 April 1680, the Brief of Clement XI, *Dudum felicis,* 7 Dec. 1703, the decree of Clement XII, 16 April 1736, and several constitutions of Benedict XIV.[6]

[1] *Collectanea Constitutionum, Decretorum, Indultorum ac Instructionum Sanctae Sedis ad usum operariorum apostolicorum Societatis Missionum ad Exteros* (Parisiis: Typis Georges Chamerot, 1880), n. 163 (hereafter cited *Coll. Soc. Miss.*).

[2] De Martinis, *Ius Pontificium de Propaganda Fide* (*Pars Prima,* 7 vols. in 8, Romae, 1888-1897; *Pars Secunda,* 1 vol., Romae,1909), *Pars I,* vol. 1, p. 304 (hereafter cited *Ius Pont.*).

[3] *Ius Pont, Pars* I, vol. 1, p. 313.

[4] *Collectanea Sacrae Congregationis de Propaganda Fide* (2 vols., Romae: Typographia Polyglotta S. C. P. F., 1907), nos. 186, 187 (hereafter cited *Coll.* S. C. P. F.).

[5] *Bullarum Diplomatum et Privilegiorum Sanctorum Romanorum Pontificum Taurinensis editio* (25 vols., Augustae Taurinorum, 1857-1872), VII, 242-248 (hereafter cited *Bull. Rom.*).

[6] Cf. S. C. P. F., instr., 23 nov. 1845—*Codicis Iuris Canonici Fontes Emi Petri Card. Gasparri editi* (9 vols., Romae-Civitate Vaticana: Typis Polyglottis Vaticanis, 1923-1939; Vols. VII, VIII, IX, ed. *cura et studio Emi Iustiniani Card. Serédi*), n. 4816 (hereafter cited *Fontes*).

The decrees thus far mentioned were rather general in nature. They insisted on the obligation of the Vicars to train a native clergy and took for granted that the norms enunciated by the Council of Trent would be wisely applied to the conditions of the missions. Besides these general decrees, however, there also were instructions which treated of special problems of administration. A decree of Clement XIII, 18 Jan. 1767, gave to the Vicar Apostolic of Siam, as to the superior of the seminary existing there, the faculty to bind by oath those entering the college, and those already in the college, to work only in the French missions of China and other regions of the Far East, so that no one could transfer to another mission or enter any religious institute, even the Jesuits, without the permission of the same Vicar Apostolic.[7]

A decree of Clement XIV, 6 Jan. 1771, ordered this oath to be enforced, and declared that under pain of nullity no student of the college could be professed in a religious order, and any superior who attempted to receive one of the said students into an order became *ipso facto* suspended from the use of his faculties. The superior of the seminary was given the faculties however to dispense from the oath in cases of urgent necessity, but for six times only. When this number of dispensations had been given, he needed to have recourse to the Holy See for a renewal of the faculty.[8] A decree of the Sacred Congregation for the Propagation of the Faith, 28 Jan. 1771, throws light on the office of rector in a central seminary. In this decree, the Congregation confirmed several privileges asked for by the rector of the Seminary of Pondicherry and approved by the Holy Father, Clement XIV. Thus within the walls of the seminary the rector had pastoral rights over his subjects, and as soon as he was elected had the necessary jurisdiction to administer the sacraments. If a Bishop or Vicar Apostolic of the French mis-

[7] *Coll. Soc. Miss.*, n. 172.

[8] *Coll. Soc. Miss.*, n. 173. The seminary that for many years existed in Siam had in this year, 1771, been transferred to Pondicherry, India.

sions was in residence at the college, the rector could permit him to confirm the students, promote them to orders, and exercise other *pontificalia,* with the permission however of the local Ordinary. The rector had the faculty to approve other missioners as prefects for the college. The rector and missioners living in the college could read prohibited books and keep the same, and they had faculties to absolve from cases reserved to the Holy See, but only for their subjects in the seminary.[9]

Finally on May 10, 1775, Pius VI, in a letter to the Vicars Apostolic of Tonkin, Ssu-ch'uan (Szechwan), Cochin-China and the directors of the seminary of the Paris Foreign Mission Society, encouraged the founding of additional seminaries in these regions. The central seminary, once situated in Siam but later located in Pondicherry, received students from China, Tonkin, Cochin-China, Cambodia and Siam. Besides this general seminary the Pope urged each Vicar Apostolic to have in his own territory a special seminary for the formation of the secular clergy. Multiplied colleges and distributed students would make for greater security in time of persecution, and thus it was not to be feared that persecution in one region would stop the missionary work in all regions.[10]

### *Synod of Ssu-ch'uan (Szechwan)*

The most important particular legislation of this period was that of the Synod of Ssu-ch'uan. This Synod was held in the city of Ch'ung-ch'ing (Chungking), Sept. 2-9, 1803, and presided over by Gabriel Taurinus Dufresse, Vicar Apostolic of Ssu-ch'uan and Administrator of the provinces of Yün-nan and Kuei-chou (Kweichow). Chapter eight of the decrees of this synod concerned the sacrament of orders. The following decrees are of interest to all who wish to

[9] *Coll. Soc. Miss.*, n. 174. The Latin terms "*domestici et commensales,*" used in this decree, seem best rendered in the English with the word *subjects,*—literally, those living and working in the seminary.

[10] *Coll. Soc. Miss.*, n. 175.

understand the development of seminary legislation in China.

I. When a boy asks to go to the Seminary, the missioner shall examine him and test the vocation of the boy for a period of one or two years before he informs the Vicar Apostolic that the boy wishes to be admitted to the seminary.

II. The boy must be 14 years of age before he can be admitted. He must also be tried for a month or two by us or by another priest appointed by us, to see if he has the requisite qualities and aptitude for study.

III. Latin, sacred Theology and other studies are to be taken. Twice a year examinations are to be held on the matter covered the previous semester. Every year or at least every second year the seminary must send a report to the Vicar Apostolic on the progress of each boy in learning and virtue.

IV. When the time is ripe, in the judgment of the rector, each boy must take the customary oath to serve this mission only and not to transfer to another mission. Otherwise the boy is to be dismissed. The Rector of the seminary is hereby given faculties to receive this oath from the students. If however the central seminary outside of our districts is restored, then to the oath is added also the clause of going here by the command of the Vicar Apostolic and remaining until commanded to return to one's own province.

VI. It is better to have a few good and learned priests than to have many bad and ignorant ones who by their depravity and ignorance offer danger, not salvation, to the people. Therefore none should be presented for sacred orders and especially for the priesthood, but those who after a long probation in the seminary are commended for wisdom, good morals, justice, chastity, and competent learning.

VII. After the course in sacred theology is completed, but before promotion to the priesthood, the cleric must, at least for a year, unless the Vicar Apostolic decides otherwise, exercise the office of catechist in the mission of one of the European missioners. The missioner will also see to it that he is an aid to the student, so that the latter will make progress in ecclesiastical discipline and theological learning.[11]

The Synod of Ssu-ch'uan was approved by the Sacred Congregation for the Propagation of the Faith in 1822, the great delay being due to the disastrous conditions in Europe.[12] The decrees of this synod remained the most important body of particular law concerning China until the celebration of the First (Plenary) Council of China in 1924. The copious references made to the Synod by the Fathers of the council show how great an influence the decrees of this synod enjoyed, even more than 100 years after their enactment.

### ARTICLE 2. FROM 1845 TO THE CODE OF CANON LAW

In 1845 the Sacred Congregation for the Propagation of the Faith issued an instruction to all Ordinaries of missions. It dealt primarily with the duty of the Bishops and Vicars Apostolic to establish seminaries. This instruction recalled the various decrees of the Popes and of the Congregation from the time of its founding down to the present, to show that the training of a native clergy had always been the first object of sending vicars into those remote regions. Having reviewed all the legislation of the past two centuries, the Congregation again insisted that the first duty of the mission Ordinaries is to form a native clergy. To this end it was necessary to erect seminaries in which the students could be trained and proven. The native clerics needed to be formed in such wise that, in accordance with the wishes of the Holy See, they might become fit for every ecclesiastical office, even that of governing the missions. Therefore to be rejected and altogether abrogated was the custom of lowering the native priests to the condition of a sort of secondary clergy. On the contrary, the rule was to be prudently intro-

[11] *Acta et Decreta Sacrorum Conciliorum Recentiorum, Collectio Lacensis* (7 vols., Freiburgi Brisgoviae: Herder, 1870-1892), VI, 618-620 (hereafter cited *Coll. Lacensis*).

[12] S. C. P. F., Epistola ... de Synodi approbatione, 29 iun. 1822—*Coll. Lacensis*, VI, 638-640.

duced, namely, that among the missioners, were they native or European, honors, offices, positions, and dignities were to be given to those who had served the mission the longest, all other considerations of course being equal.[13]

Again, in 1877, the Sacred Congregation dealt with the subject of seminaries in an instruction to the Vicars and Prefects of the missions. These latter were asked to report on whether a seminary existed in their mission, on whether seminarians were kept separate from lay students, on the nature of the studies required of them, and on whether the regulations of the Council of Trent were observed in whole or in part. They were to indicate also under whose direction the seminary had been placed, and, finally, if no seminary existed whether one could somehow be erected, or whether the deficiency could be made good in some other way.[14]

### *Instruction of 1883*

The final and basic pre-Code legislation for the constitution and administration of seminaries in China is part of a lengthy instruction of the Sacred Congregation for the Propagation of the Faith to the Vicars Apostolic of China, 18 Oct. 1883. It was the purpose of the fourth part of this instruction to apply to the conditions of the Chinese missions the decree of the Council of Trent on seminaries. It contained the following provisions:

> 1. [Selection of candidates]. According to the decrees of the Council of Trent a certain number of boys are to be provided for and educated in the seminary. Now that the Vicar Apostolic may inform himself of the good character of a boy, let the rules of the synod of Szechwan be observed. The missioner shall have the boy serve at the altar for a few years—and if possible even have the boy live with him, so that he may learn more about his character. Then the missioner may propose the new

[13] S. C. P. F., instr., 23 nov. 1845—*Fontes*, n. 4816; *Coll. S. C. P. F.*, n. 1002.

[14] S. C. P. F., instr., 1 iun. 1877—*Fontes*, n. 4891; *Coll. S. C. P. F.*, n. 1473.

student to the Vicar Apostolic for admission into the preparatory school. The boy must be 12 years of age, or at the very least 10, and ordinarily not more than 14. The student shall remain in the seminary for two years, as it were on probation, and, if he is found fit, may be enrolled as a member of the college.

2. [Preparatory Seminary]. It is good to educate these boys in a school distinct from other schools, and better, if as is already done in many missions, in a preparatory seminary distinct from the major seminary.

3. [Regional Seminaries]. Since however many Vicariates in China have not even the shadow of a seminary and have not the means at hand to erect one, lest they be deprived of this salutary institution, the Congregation commends to the Prefects of the missions that by common agreement they institute one or more central or provincial seminaries in the single regions, and thus make it easier to get together sufficient teachers and moderators, and the money and other things necessary for the constitution of the seminary. This is indeed the mind of the Fathers of Trent, for they decreed that if the churches in some province were too poor to erect their own seminaries, then the provincial synod or the metropolitan with his two oldest suffragans should erect one or more seminaries in the metropolitan see or in some other more convenient place, so that, being supported by the funds of each church concerned, this seminary could educate the boys of all the churches too poor to have their own colleges.

4. [The Major Seminary]. The Holy Council also strictly commanded that laymen be in no wise received into the major seminary, and as soon as it is evident that one of the students has not an ecclesiastical vocation, he is to be expelled from the college, so that it can be said to be a perpetual seminary of the ministers of God.

5. [Officials of the Seminary]. That the work of the seminary be carried out efficiently it is necessary that the Vicars Apostolic see to it that the priests to whom the rule of the seminary is committed be excused from all other works of the ministry.

Let them also assign to the seminary a spiritual director whose duty it shall be to form the students in a solid spiritual life.

6. [Studies]. Concerning the course of studies, let the decrees of the Council of Trent be adhered to. The Congregation thinks it good, however, to call special attention to a few matters which are of importance for China. In the first place, let the Vicars and Prefects of the single regions depute, by common consent, learned and expert men to treat of the course of studies and to submit their ideas to the Bishops, who shall discuss them in the forthcoming synods. Let them especially consider the textbooks to be used; whether the Latin authors of the Golden Age are to be given indiscriminately to the students, whether and how the classical Chinese authors are to be studied. Let them however give special consideration to the question of authors in rational philosophy and sacred Theology. The Congregation is happy to see that many of the Fathers are solicitous about having introduced into their schools the philosophy taught according to the method of St. Thomas. This spirit is to be commended and it would be praiseworthy for the above mentioned men to consider just how this wish can be reduced to practice, indicating the authors who are best suited to the circumstances of place and the aptitude of the students. Likewise let them consider how in philosophy and theology the errors of Chinese philosophy and religion are to be refuted. It would be opportune to compose a work which expressly refutes these errors, so that the students studying for the priesthood will be formed into staunch apologists able to refute the errors of their nation. Finally and especially, in the treatise on the Church [*de Ecclesia*], teach the students the validity of and the reasons for the doctrine of the primacy of the Roman Pontiff, and see to it that they are imbued with a deep love and reverence for the Roman Church.

8. [Funds]. Concerning the funds necessary to erect the seminary and support the students, since the things decreed by the Fathers of the Council of Trent cannot be carried out in the places of the

missions, the Congregation commends to all Vicars Apostolic that in using the funds of the mission, they give to the seminary the first portion after the necessary sustenance of the missioners.

9. [Ordinations]. In ordaining clerics to the priesthood, let the Vicars remember the words of the Synod of Szechwan, namely, that no one be promoted to sacred orders until after a long period of probation in the seminary. No one is therefore to be ordained unless he be commended by the acquisition of sufficient learning, heavenly wisdom, good morals, and a long observance of justice and chastity. Let the Vicars not hesitate to put off the ordination beyond the common age (24) if they think it better or necessary.

Now if the Superiors of the Chinese missions reduce all these things to practice, in as far as the difficulties of place and time will permit, they will no doubt reap abundant fruits from their colleges of the ministers of God.[15]

This instruction of the Sacred Congregation is the last important piece of legislation on seminaries in China before the new Code of Canon Law. The canons of the Code of course apply to China as well as to the rest of the Latin Church. The Code gives us a complete legislation on seminaries in canons 1352 to 1371. These canons may be outlined as follows:

Right of the Church to establish seminaries—can. 1352.
Vocations to the priesthood—can. 1353.
Duty of Bishops to institute seminaries—can. 1354.
Economic support—canons 1355, 1356, 1362.
Administration:
- rights and duties of the Bishop—can. 1357;
- the rector and officials—canons 1358, 1360, 1361, 1366, 1369;
- the boards—can. 1359;
- admission to the seminary—can. 1363.

Studies:

[15] S. C. P. F., instr., 18 oct. 1883, IV, nos. 1-9—*Fontes*, n. 4903; *Coll. S. C. P. F.*, n. 1606.

in the minor seminary—can. 1364;
in the major seminary—can. 1365;
professors—can. 1366;
exceptional cases—can. 1370.
Religious exercises—can. 1367.
Jurisdiction and exemption—can. 1368.
Dismissal—can. 1371.

The canons which immediately pertain to this dissertation are canons 1354, § 3, and 1357, § 4. "If it is impossible to establish a diocesan seminary or to get adequate training, especially in philosophy and theology, in the one which is established, the Bishop should send his students to another seminary, unless an interdiocesan or regional seminary has been established by papal authority."[16] And, the "entire management and administration of an interdiocesan or regional seminary is governed by rules established by the Holy See."[17] The treatment of these two canons shall follow in the second part of this work.

### ARTICLE 3. THE FIRST PLENARY COUNCIL OF CHINA

The First Plenary Council of China was held at Hsü-chia-hui (Zi-ka-wei), Shang-hai, from May 14 to June 12, 1924. The decrees were approved by the Sacred Congregation for the Propagation of the Faith on June 12, 1928. The council's special purpose was the application of the canons of the Code of Canon Law to China, and the discussion of the things that would help the evangelization of that country. The council abrogated the laws of previous synods, and also all custom and particular precepts contrary to the decrees now enacted, unless of course the contrary was expressly stated.[18] Book IV of the decrees and norms of this

[16] Can. 1354, § 3—*Codex Iuris Canonici Pii X Pontificis Maximi iussu digestus Benedicti Papae XV auctoritate promulgatus* (Romae: Typis Polyglottis Vaticanis, 1917).

[17] Can. 1357, § 4.

[18] *Primum Concilium Sinense—Acta—Decreta et Normae—Vota, etc.* (Zi-ka-wei: Typographia Missionis Catholicae, 1929), *Decreta et Normae*, nos. 11-13 (hereafter cited *PCS*—all numbers refer to the *Decreta et Normae* unless the contrary be stated).

council deals with the evangelization of the Chinese people. Of this book, the fourth title concerns the formation of the native clergy. The decrees of this title cover most of the canons of the Code of Canon Law in regard to the constitution and administration of seminaries. The writer shall restrict himself to the making of a summary report.[19]

Numbers 642-648 of the decrees are, as it were, an introduction to the seminary legislation. They repeat the exhortations of the apostolic letter *Maximum illud* of Benedict XV, concerning the formation of a native clergy. Vocations to the priestly and religious life are therefore encouraged, and indication is given that among the things necessary for the Vicariate the seminary should hold the first place.

Chapter I. The Preparatory College.—This chapter covers number 649 to 651, and repeats the prescriptions of canons 1353, 1363, § 1, and 1364, 1°, 3°.

Chapter II. Concerning the Seminary in General.—This chapter covers admission to and dismissal from the seminary, and except for a few minor additions repeats the doctrine of canons 1354, §§ 1, 2, 1363, §§ 1, 2, 3, and 1371. The numbers of the decrees of the council are 652 to 657. Number 654 adds that students for the priesthood should be sought not only from families of more humble position, but also from families conspicuous for noble birth, public office, or wealth.

Chapter III. Duties of the Ordinary.—Number 658 concerns the duty of general administration as does canon 1357, §§ 1, 2, 3, but adds that the Ordinary who has students in other seminaries or in central or regional seminaries is bound by the same duties of vigilance, so that no one be promoted to sacred orders unless proof is had of his integrity of life and competent learning. Number 659 states that the Ordinary with the advice of the consultors shall determine the courses of studies as well as the textbooks and authors, and that the professors are not allowed to change these things without consulting the Ordinary.

[19] *PCS*, nos. 642-681.

Chapter IV. Officials and Professors.—Number 660 to 663 treat of the same material and re-state the prescripts of canons 1358, 1360, 1361, and 891. However, in regard to canon 1358, namely that each seminary should have a rector, professors, a procurator, two ordinary confessors and a spiritual director, number 660 adds that "in the missions this canon shall be observed as well as it can be." Number 664 admits that it is very desirable to have the two boards of governors mentioned in canon 1359, but that if this be impossible, as it is because of lack of missioners, then let the Ordinary obtain the same ends as above (discipline and administration of temporalities) by using his consultors, and let him take advice from them in matters of greater moment. Finally, number 665 encourages the rectors of the various seminaries to meet in conventions to discuss their common problems.

Chapter V. Internal Discipline.—Number 666 is the same as canon 1367, namely, it enumerates the practices of piety to be carried out in the seminary. But number 667 adds a daily visit to the Blessed Sacrament, daily spiritual reading, the particular examen, the recitation of the rosary, all in common, and if it be at all possible also a monthly day of recollection. Number 668 repeats canon 1369, namely, that the rector and officials must be vigilant concerning piety, discipline, and learning, and number 669 wisely adds that they should not permit the students to while away the whole time of recreation in idleness and inactivity, but see to it that the students are occupied in various bodily exercises, as, for instance, in games, garden work and gymnastics.

Chapter VI. Examinations.—This chapter consists of but one number, that is, number 670, and the gist of the decree is that examinations should be held once a year at least, and much better twice a year, namely at the end of each semester.

Chapter VII. The Minor Seminary.—According to number 671, the students are not to be admitted to the seminary unless they have first finished the studies in the preparatory school. Moreover, the length of the studies to be undertaken in the minor seminary shall be determined by the Ordinary with the advice of the consultors. Number 672 repeats canon 1364 with reference to the studies to be taken in the minor seminary, but very wisely adds that the Latin language ought to be taught in such wise that the students become duly prepared for the study of philosophy and theology; therefore to be studied are the classical authors of the golden age, the Fathers, the liturgical hymns, and the lessons of the Roman Breviary.

Chapter VIII. The Major Seminary.—The professors and the courses of study in philosophy and theology are covered by numbers 673-676, which correspond to canons 1365, 1366, and 1370. Number 674 adds that the Ordinaries should give opportunity for further study to those who have the necessary talents and health. With regard to the funds, the council does not repeat the prescriptions of the canons of the Code, because these things cannot be accomplished in the missions. The parents of the boys are asked to pay the expenses in so far as their means allow (n. 677), and benefactors are asked not to attach burdensome conditions when founding burses or giving alms. Finally, number 679 merely repeats canon 1362 with reference to the use of revenues derived from endowments for both the minor and major seminary. And if the Vicar Apostolic cannot erect a major seminary of his own, he shall send his students to another seminary, or to a central or regional seminary. (n. 680—can. 1354, § 3).

Chapter IX. Regional Seminaries.—This chapter consists of number 681 and states that the council accepts the instructions and norms which the Congregation for the Propagation of the Faith shall give for the erection and administration of regional seminaries.

From this summary report of the decrees of the council it is evident that the canons of the Code are applied to the conditions of the missions. Canons 1355 and 1356 are omitted. The reason is evident. They cannot be applied to conditions in China. The support of the seminary will *in praxi* be ruled mainly by the instruction of 1883—the Vicars and Prefects are commanded that in the use of the funds given to the mission or held by the mission, they use for the seminary the first portion after the necessary sustenance of the missioners.[20]

### *Résume*

In closing this chapter the writer makes a few observations in retrospect. First of all, the basic legislation for seminaries, even in China, was the decree of the Council of Trent on seminaries. The constitutions of the Popes and the instructions of the Sacred Congregation insist on its observance and apply its prescriptions to the conditions of the Chinese missions. Conditions in China make it necessary to depart from the common law in a number of points. The decree of the Council of Trent, and later the canons of the Code, concerning funds are impractical for China, since the seminary must be maintained from the common funds of the mission. Likewise, the condition of lower education in China makes it feasible to have a preparatory school distinct from and prior to the minor seminary. Again, because of lack of means and men the major seminary in China will usually be not diocesan but regional.

It is to be noted that there is not much legislation enacted specifically for regional seminaries. Legislation is rather for seminaries in general, and special mention is made of regional seminaries as a remedy when diocesan seminaries cannot be established. Most of the legislation for regional seminaries was made after the appearance of the Code of Canon Law.

Finally it must be noted that neither the Council of Trent, nor the decrees of the Congregation for the Propagation of the Faith, especially the most important one of 1883, nor the instruction of the same Congregation to the Bishops of India, 28 Aug. 1893[21]—therefore none of the three sources

[20] S. C. P. F., instr., 18 oct. 1883, IV, n. 8—*Fontes*, n. 4903.
[21] *Fontes*, n. 4928.

mentioned in the footnotes to the Code of Canon Law under canon 1354, § 3—demand that the erection of a regional seminary be reserved exclusively to the Holy See. On the contrary, it is evident from these decrees that regional seminaries could be erected by the provincial synods as well as by the common agreement of the Vicars and Prefects of the regions interested in the project. It should also be noted that the Code of Canon Law does not carry any footnote to canon 1357, § 4, which canon states that the rule and administration of regional seminaries are governed by the norms established by the Holy See.[22]

[22] On this point confer Masarei, *De Missionum Institutione ac de Relationibus inter Superiores Missionum et Superiores Religiosos* (Romae: Apud Institutum Graphicum Tiberinum, 1940), p. 274 (hereafter cited *De Missionum Institutione*); and also Vermeersch—Creusen, *Epitome Iuris Canonici* (6. ed., 3 vols., Mechlinae: H. Dessain, 1937-1946), II, 707 (hereafter cited *Epitome*).

# CHAPTER III

## ACTUAL ESTABLISHMENT OF REGIONAL SEMINARIES IN CHINA

### ARTICLE 1. THE MOVEMENT TOWARD REGIONAL SEMINARIES

Several central seminaries serving the Chinese missions had existed in Europe and in the Far East for several centuries. Witness for instance the seminary of the Paris Foreign Mission Society at Siam—Pondicherry—Penang. However, the great development of regional seminaries in China dates from the promulgation of the new Code of Canon Law. Pope Benedict XV in his apostolic letter *Maximum illud* stated that the methods used in the educating of the native clergy had up to the present time been defective and faulty. The remedy had to consist in well regulated seminaries either for the single regions or for several dioceses together. "We command the Sacred Congregation for the Propagation of the Faith to establish seminaries wherever there is need for the benefit of the single regions or for several dioceses simultaneously, and to see to the proper management of those that are already founded."[1]

Thus also Pope Pius XI declared that, if the Vicars and Prefects Apostolic did not work with all energy to build up a native clergy, their apostolate would not only be handicapped, but would prove an obstacle to the establishment of the Church in those countries. It was necessary to supply the territories of the missions with as many native priests as would prove sufficient by themselves for the extension of the boundaries of Christianity and for the government

[1] Benedictus XV, ep. apost. *Maximum illud,* 30 nov. 1919—*Acta Apostolicae Sedis* (Romae, 1909—), XI (1919), 440-445 ( hereafter cited *AAS*); *Sylloge Praecipuorum Documentorum Recentium Summorum Pontificum et S. Congregationis de Propaganda Fide necnon Aliarum SS. Congregationum Romanarum ad Usum Missionariorum* (Romae: Typis Polyglottis Vaticanis, 1939), n. 74 (hereafter cited *Sylloge*).

of the community of the faithful, without having to depend upon the help of the foreign clergy. The Pontiff rejoiced in the knowledge that seminaries had already been erected in central locations between neighboring missions which were entrusted to the same missionary order or congregation. To these seminaries the Vicars and Prefects were to send their clerics and maintain them at their own expense, to receive them back one day as ordained priests prepared for the ministry. What therefore had been done here and there by some, the Pontiff commanded to be done by all, so that no native who gave promise needed to be kept away from the priesthood, provided he gave signs of a true vocation.[2]

### *Apostolic Visitation*

The practical application of these directives to China was made early in the 1920's. With the approval of Pope Benedict XV, the Sacred Congregation for the Propagation of the Faith instituted an apostolic visitation of China through the ministry of Bishop Jean-Baptiste Budes de Guébriant, M.E.P., Vicar Apostolic of Kuang-chou (Canton). The decree for the visitation was issued on the 22nd of July, 1919, and the visitation took place from September 1919 to March 1920.[3]

The Apostolic Visitor received instructions to give special attention to the matter of seminaries and the formation of the native clergy. "See what manner of care is taken in selecting vocations and in the intellectual and moral education of the students. What ought to be improved, what things reformed, especially as to the program of studies, so that the education of the Chinese clergy might be made more adequate. How practical provision can be made for the erection of regional seminaries, and for sending the best

[2] Pius XI, litt. encycl. *Rerum Ecclesiae,* 28 febr. 1926—*AAS,* XVIII (1926), 65-83; *Sylloge,* n. 120.

[3] S. C. P. F., decr., 22 iul. 1919— *Archivum S. C. P. F.,* Sinae—Negotia Communia, a. 1919.

students to Rome in order to complete their studies there according to the express desire of the Supreme Pontiff."[4]

After the visitation the Apostolic Visitor submitted his views concerning regional seminaries to the Congregation in a note entitled: "Note Concerning a Regional Seminary for Central and North China." According to this note, Bishop de Guébriant distinguished two categories of missions which should not be obliged to send their students to a common seminary. In the first category were the missions which belonged to the same religious institute and really wished to begin a central seminary of their own. Such were perhaps the Belgian mission of the Scheut Fathers and the Italian missions of Ho-nan. The second category comprised missions which, thanks to their zeal, their resources, their development, had already put their seminaries on a solid footing. Such seminaries existed in Chiang-nan (Kiangnan),[5] Che-chiang (Chekiang), Shan-tung, Chih-li, Mongolia, Ssu-ch'uan (Szechwan), etc. There was yet a third category: missions which did not have, and would not have for some time to come, an adequate seminary for philosophy and theology. It would be chimerical to expect that these missions, even if pressed by Rome, would agree among themselves to establish a common seminary. It seems therefore that the only means, costly but effective, would be to establish in China, and in a well-chosen locality easy of access, a regional seminary by Pontifical authority, to which the undeveloped missions should and all the missions could send their students. Chih-fou (Chefoo) in North Shan-tung seemed for many reasons (climate, communications, freedom from powerful missions) a well-chosen place. But if the direction of the seminary were given to one of the institutes exercising the ministry in China, jealousies and complaints would have

[4] S. C. P. F., instr., 22 iul. 1919, ad B, V°—*Archivum S. C. P. F.*, n. 1697/19, rub. 130.

[5] The name Chiang-nan designated a vice-royalty or administrative unit embracing the civil provinces of Chiang-su (Kiangsu) and Anhui (Anhwei), ruled by a viceroy or governor general, under whose jurisdiction were the governors of the two provinces.

to be expected. It was therefore suggested that the Institute of St. Sulpice be invited to administer the seminary. They would probably contribute to the foundation of the seminary, and their contribution plus that of the several missions and the help given by the Sacred Congregation for the Propagation of the Faith would allow an early realization of the project.[6]

These recommendations of Bishop de Guébriant were considered fully in a plenary congregation (meeting) of the Sacred Congregation in July of 1922. Concerning seminaries the following matters were decided:

1. The opinions of Bishop de Guébriant having been considered, the Congregation has already drawn up norms for the administration of regional seminaries and has attempted to have some of these seminaries erected. For this purpose the Congregation has encouraged the Vicariates entrusted to the same religious institute to come to some agreement. But up until the present time only one regional seminary has been erected—that of Ta-t'ung for the missions committed to the Scheut Fathers in the northern provinces of China.

2. The Friars Minor seem also to have come to an agreement. They hope to erect a regional seminary at Wu-ch'ang, Hu-pei (Hupeh) province. The Congregation has sent them the norms of administration and now the seminary has opened provisionally. Perhaps by next year it shall be definitely established.

3. Lately, the Lazarists made known their intention of erecting a regional seminary for the four vicariates of the civil province of Chiang-hsi (Kiangsi) and another for the two vicariates of the province of Che-chiang (Chekiang). To them therefore the Congregation has also sent the norms of administration.[7]

[6] "Note Relative à un Seminaire Regional pour la Chine du Centre et du Nord," 1 iunii 1920—*Archivum S.C.P.F.*, n. 2378/20 prot., rub. 130.

[7] The major seminary of Nan-ch'ang in the civil province of Chiang-hsi, and the common seminary of Ning-po in the civil province of

4. The negotiations for the erection of a central seminary in Hsiang-kang (Hongkong), for the Vicariate of Hsiang-kang and the Vicariates of North Fu-chien (North Fukien) and Hsia-men (Amoy), have had no results because of lack of funds. Thus also the Milan Foreign Mission Society cannot yet erect a regional seminary for their three vicariates in the civil province of Ho-nan.[8]

5. For the vicariates situated in southern China the opinion is approved by which the seminary at Penang be considered the central seminary for the missions of southern China and the Islands. Besides, all Ordinaries of the Paris Foreign Mission Society in China may send their students here. The Sacred Congregation now expects information and proposals for the nomination of the officials and professors and for the redaction of the programs (of study and discipline)—then this proposition will be expedited.[9]

*Observations*

From what has been related above, one may draw a few important conclusions which furnish valuable information on regional seminaries in China. First of all, the Visitor Apostolic distinguished in China a category of missions entrusted to the same religious or missionary institute. If these missions wished to erect a common seminary, Bishop de Guébriant believed the seminary should be approved. The Sacred Congregation expressly praised these seminaries, and in later years declared many of them to be canonically erected as regional seminaries. Pope Pius XI in

Che-chiang, actually do receive students from other missions, but have never obtained canonical erection into regional seminaries.

[8] These seminaries were however erected at a later date, namely, in 1926, the Regional Seminary of Hsiang-kang, and, in 1932, the Regional Seminary of K'ai-feng.

[9] S. C. P. F., C. G., 31 iul. 1922—*Archivum S. C. P. F.*, n. 1714/22 prot., rub. 130. The "Rules of the General Seminary of the Paris Foreign Mission Society at Penang" were approved by the Sacred Congregation in 1926, and in 1934 the seminary was subjected to the *Normae* of 1934.

the encyclical letter *Rerum Ecclesiae* also praised and approved these regional seminaries and commanded that more of them be established.[10]

The second category of missions have seminaries of their own, and such as are considered adequate for a full training of the native clergy. However, the Sacred Congregation during the years 1920-1946 encouraged many such seminaries to become re-established as regional seminaries in order to achieve a better all-around administration and program of studies. Therefore Bishop de Guébriant's recommendations were not followed in this point.

The third category of missions are those which are unable to have their own diocesan seminary and are unwilling or unable to agree to the erection of a regional seminary for the several missions. For these, Bishop de Guébriant proposed that a regional seminary be erected in Chih-fou (Chefoo), Shan-tung province, where the students of the missions in central and northern China were to be educated. The Visitor's letter also suggested that missions of this third category in south China send their students to the general seminary at Penang, Malacca, which seminary was managed by the Paris Foreign Mission Society. The Congregation of the Propagation of the Faith allowed the missions of south China to send their students to the seminary at Penang, and also allowed all Ordinaries of the Paris Foreign Mission Society in China to consider this their central seminary. In 1926, however, the Regional Seminary of Hsiang-kang (Hongkong) was also established for the missions of south China.

The recommendation to establish a regional seminary at Chih-fou (Chefoo) for the missions of the central and northern provinces of China was never acted upon, and no such seminary was ever established. The policy mainly followed was the one that received expression in Bishop de Guébriant's first recommendation. Several missions in the care of one and the same religious or missionary institute were

[10] Pius XI, litt. encycl. *Rerum Ecclesiae*, 28 febr. 1926—*Syllogue*, n. 120.

allowed to band together to erect a regional seminary for their missions. This policy was somewhat modified through the fact that regional seminaries committed to one religious institute often received students from missions entrusted to other institutes or to the native secular clergy, so that the seminaries were not merely general seminaries for the missions of one order or congregation but truly regional seminaries for the region, province or provinces concerned.

With regard to terminology, it may be asked which seminaries ought to be called regional in the canonical sense of the word. Mission periodicals often confuse the terms regional, central, general, common, intermissional, and so forth. At times these terms are taken to mean one and the same thing, at other times not. In a letter to the Cardinal Prefect of the Congregation for the Propagation of the Faith, Monsignor Conrad Abels, Vicar Apostolic of East Mongolia (now Je-ho), stated:

> Our motherhouse of Scheut sends me a copy of the general rules that the S. C. of Propaganda has just issued for the regional seminaries of China. In the Far East we distinguish rather clearly regional seminaries from merely central seminaries. By the latter we mean institutes which admit students from any vicariate; by the former, institutes established for an entire ecclesiastical province or region, that is, in China, for one of the five regions.
>
> If your Eminence takes the word "regional" in that sense, it would be very useful that you make known to the synods preparatory to the General Synod that it is really your desire that seminaries of this nature be founded in this country.[11]

The Congregation did not embrace this distinction made by Msgr. Abels. Although it is indeed the ideal to have a regional seminary for each ecclesiastical province, yet, even up to the present, regional seminaries are considered to be

[11] From a letter of Msgr. Abels to Card. Van Rossum, 16 Sept. 1921—*Archivum S. C. P. F.*, Mongolia Orientalis, a. 1921. The missions of China had been divided into five ecclesiastical regions in 1879. Confer S. C. P. F., decr., 23 iunii 1879—*Archivum S. C. P. F.*, Acta S. C. P. F., Vol. 247, pp. 228-230.

those which are recognized as such and which are governed by special norms of the Holy See. These seminaries may perhaps accept students from several provinces; again they may accept students from several missions of one province, whereas other missions of the very same province may send their students elsewhere. The only exact terminology in this matter is, therefore, that regional seminaries are such as are thus recognized by the Holy See and are governed by the special norms of the Holy See. Other seminaries which actually receive students from several missions or from several provinces, but which are not recognized as regional seminaries by the Holy See, are properly called common, general, intermissional seminaries.[12]

### *The First Plenary Council of China*

Not long after the apostolic visitation, plans were made for the holding of the first plenary council of China. As has been noted above, this council was held in 1924. Its decrees were approved by the Sacred Congregation for the Propagation of the Faith on June 12, 1928, and were promulgated by the Apostolic Delegate on December 12, 1928.[13] As is evident, the decrees of the council have the force of law for all of China, and they treat of seminaries in the same manner as does the Code of Canon Law. The Council of China recognizes the right of each Ordinary to have his own seminary, it exhorts the Ordinaries to erect two seminaries, a major and minor seminary, but when this is impossible, especially with regard to the major seminary, then the Ordinaries must send their students to another seminary, or to a central or regional seminary, if one is at hand.[14] Regional

[12] "Seminari regionali sono tutti quelli dichiarati tali dalla Sacra Congregazione di Propaganda Fide e governati secondo il rescritto del 27—IV—1934—Prot. 1989/34. I seminari inter-territoriali sono seminari non dichiarati regionali dalla S. C. di P. F., che di fatto contano studenti provenienti da due o più territori ecclesiastici." —*Guida delle Missioni Cattoliche* (Roma: Ed. Unione Missionaria del Clero in Italia, 1934), p. 83.

[13] *PCS, Acta,* pp. 20-22.

[14] *PCS,* nos. 652, 680.

seminaries are therefore to be erected when it is impossible to have well regulated and well staffed diocesan seminaries. In fact, however, there are very few missions which have sufficient means for the establishment of well regulated and well staffed diocesan seminaries for philosophy and theology. Therefore the Sacred Congregation has been very active in urging the constitution of regional seminaries in China.

### Article 2. The Regulations of 1921 and 1934

The first set of general regulations governing regional seminaries subject to the jurisdiction of the Congregation for the Propagation of the Faith was drawn up in 1921. These regulations were composed in Italian, and sent to regional seminaries erected at that time. As far as is known, the original text was never published. However, the Apostolic Delegate to China published a Latin translation in the *Collectanea Commissionis Synodalis,* in 1932.[15] Since some omissions occur in the Latin translation, the version which here follows is made from the Italian text.

Norms for Regional Seminaries in China[16]

I. Supreme Direction

1. The regional seminary is placed under the supreme supervision of the Sacred Congregation for the Propagation of the Faith.

2. The Ordinaries of the region shall by common agreement submit to the Sacred Congregation for the Propagation of the Faith for approval:

a) the choice of the place where the regional seminary is to be erected;

b) the rules of discipline for the seminary;

c) the program of studies, the arrangement of the branches, the scholastic *horarium,* and a list of textbooks;

[15] *Collectanea Commissionis Synodalis,* V (1932), 594-595 (hereafter cited *Coll. Comm. Syn.*).

[16] "Norme per i Seminari Regionali in Cina," S. C. P. F., 14 mart. 1921—*Archivum S. C. P. F.*, n. 3426/21 prot., rub. 8 (hereafter cited *Norme* [1921]).

d) an estimate of the seminary's income, and an appraisal of the amount of expected contributions coming from the single missions; also an estimate of the funds necessary to operate the institution.

3. a) The election of the rector pertains to the Sacred Congregation for the Propagation of the Faith, after presentation of a candidate by the Ordinaries;

b) the election of the professors shall be submitted to the same Congregation for confirmation. Likewise their dismissal shall be reported to the Sacred Congregation for ratification.

4. All students of philosophy and theology in the region must be sent to the seminary; and the Ordinaries may not withdraw them from this seminary in order to educate them in some other place, without the permission of the Congregation for the Propagation of the Faith.

### II. Rights and Duties of the Ordinaries of the Region

5. Ordinary jurisdiction over the regional seminary is held by all the Ordinaries of the region, who shall exercise it through the ministry of the Ordinary of the place where the seminary is erected.

6. a) Each year they shall meet to treat of the things relating to the discipline, studies, and economic administration of the institute; and to this end they shall examine the written report which the rector of the seminary shall present concerning these things;

b) the Bishop of the place shall preside at this annual meeting, or, in his absence, the senior of the Ordinaries; and another Ordinary, namely the youngest by way of nomination, shall act as secretary.

7. It shall be the right of the Ordinaries to elect and to dismiss, by common agreement, the spiritual director, the procurator, and the other officials and professors of the seminary. In these things they should hear the opinion of the rector of the seminary.

8. The Ordinaries may ordain their own subjects, after the completion of studies, in their own proper mission, or they may grant dimissorial let-

ters so that their subjects may be ordained by the Ordinary of the place where the seminary is located.

III. Rights and Duties of the Local Ordinary

9. It is the exclusive right of the local Ordinary to exercise vigilance concerning the observance of the rules of the institute, the scholastic program, and the entire administration of the seminary. He also has the right to put into execution the resolutions agreed upon in the annual meeting of the Ordinaries of the region.

IV. Rights and Duties of the Rector

10. He is the superior of the seminary, and the entire teaching and governing staff are dependent upon him. The Ordinary of the place shall communicate the resolutions concerning the rule of the institute to the rector, and the rector shall see to it that he is in frequent communication with the local Ordinary. Each year he shall present to the meeting of the Bishops, the spiritual and economic report of the institute, as has been mentioned in article 6, a) above. Periodically, during the course of the year, he shall send to the individual Ordinaries an accurate account of the conduct and progress in study of their respective students.

11. The seminary with its adjacent property is exempt from the jurisdiction of the quasi-pastor; the parochial duties compatible with the nature of a pious institute are entrusted to the rector of the seminary, who indeed shall exercise them through the agency of the spiritual director.

12. Before ordinations it shall be the duty of the rector to provide for the dispatching and collecting of the necessary documents; and, after making a record of them, he shall transmit them to the Ordinaries, and take care also to inquire early as to their intentions concerning the place where the ordination of each student is to take place.

### *A Development*

The norms of 1921 were imposed on regional seminaries founded in these early years. These norms were evidently meant to meet a situation in which the Vicars Apostolic of the same religious or missionary institute agreed to erect a regional seminary for their missions, and the administration of the seminary was set up in such a way that the Congregation dealt directly with the Ordinaries of the region. The board of Ordinaries had the immediate responsibility for the seminary, and it carried on its work through the agency of the rector who had been chosen by them and presented by them to the Sacred Congregation for his definite appointment.

In the course of time it seemed better to the Congregation to entrust the ordinary administration of the seminary to a religious or missionary institute. Accordingly there resulted another set of regulations, issued in 1934, and drawn up in such wise as to give the administration of the regional seminary to a religious institute. New seminaries were thenceforth to be erected according to the tenor of these norms, and the seminaries following the regulations of 1921 were to become re-organized according to the later norms. One seminary however, which had been entrusted to the native secular clergy, continued to function according to the norms of 1921.

The regulations of 1934 are the following:

Regulations for Regional Seminaries
Entrusted to Religious or Missionary Institutes[17]

I. Supreme Direction

1. The regional seminary belongs to the Holy See, which entrusts the government of it to a religious or missionary institute under the supreme direction of the Sacred Congregation for the Propagation of the Faith. To the institute are committed

[17] Italian text: "Norme per i Seminari Regionali Affidati ad Istituti Religiosi o Missionari (approvate con rescritto della Sacra Congregazione di Propaganda Fide, 27 aprile 1934, n. 1989/34 prot. con allegato)"—*Archivum S. C. P. F.*, n. 1989/34 rub. 71/3.

Latin text: "Normae pro Seminariis Regionalibus commissis Institutis religiosis vel missionalibus a Sacra Congregatione de Propaganda Fide approbatae die 27 aprilis 1934."—*Sylloge*, n. 183 (hereafter cited *Normae* [1934]).

the discipline, studies, and ordinary administration.

2. The seminary has a course of at least two years in philosophy, and of four years in theology.

3. The institute to which the direction of the regional seminary is entrusted shall submit to the Sacred Congregation for the Propagation of the Faith for approval:

a) The disciplinary regulations of the seminary;

b) the program of studies, the arrangement of the subjects, the scholastic *horarium*, and a list of textbooks.

4. a) The election of the rector of the seminary pertains to the Sacred Congregation for the Propagation of the Faith upon the presentation of a candidate by the Superior General of the institute;

b) the election of the other officials and professors pertains to the Superior General of the institute, who shall however communicate their names [that is, his appointments] to the Sacred Congregation for the Propagation of the Faith;

c) it is the right of the same Sacred Congregation to change or remove the rector of the seminary; any change made in professors or in other superiors must be communicated to the same Sacred Congregation.

5. Ordinarily all students of philosophy and theology in the region must be sent to the regional seminary; the Ordinaries may not withdraw their students from this seminary in order to educate them elsewhere without the express permission of the Sacred Congregation for the Propagation of the Faith.

6. The students of the seminary who persevere in their ecclesiastical vocation may not enter a religious institute—neither during the course of studies, nor before the lapse of three full years from their ordination to the priesthood—without the special consent of their own Ordinary and of the Holy See, without prejudice also to the provisions of canons 981, § 1, and 542 of the Code of Canon Law.

## II. Rights and Duties of the Superior General of the Institute

7. The selection of the directing and teaching staff and the distribution of offices among the officials and teachers of the seminary are committed to the care of the Superior General of the institute (without prejudice however to the provision of art. 4, a).

8. The spiritual director assigned to the students shall never be chosen from the ranks of the superiors of the seminary; and he shall maintain permanent residence within the walls of the seminary.

9. The Superior General shall come to an agreement with the Ordinaries of the region regarding the temporal [economic] administration of the seminary.

## III. Rights and Duties of the Ordinaries of the Region

10. The Ordinaries of the region may visit and correspond with their own students. They shall be free to come to the seminary in order to assist now and then at the lectures, to attend examinations, scholastic disputations, and the distribution of awards.

11. Promotion to sacred orders falls within the exclusive competence of the Ordinary of the individual students. The rector shall in good time send to the Ordinaries the necessary information regarding the piety, studies, and other qualities of those to be ordained.

12. The Ordinaries of the region shall meet every year to consider carefully all the matters relating to the discipline, piety, studies and economic administration of the seminary, and for this purpose they shall examine the written report presented by the rector of the seminary on these matters. The Bishop who is first according to the canonical rules of precedence shall preside at this meeting, the office of secretary being filled by the Ordinary most recently consecrated. At this meeting each of the Ordinaries shall approve and sign the annual spiritual and financial report of the seminary, which shall be drawn up according to the annexed outline,

and forwarded to the Sacred Congregation for the Propagation of the Faith.

13. If any observations are to be made concerning the seminary, they are as a rule to be communicated to the rector of the seminary by the local Ordinary.

### IV. Rights and Duties of the Rector of the Seminary

14. The rector is the immediate superior of the seminary, and the other officials and professors are his subordinates.

15. Each year, but without ordinarily being personally present, he shall submit to the meeting of the Bishops an accurate report of the moral and economic status of the seminary.

16. The seminary with its adjacent property is exempt from the jurisdiction of the local pastor; the parochial duties compatible with the nature of a pious institute belong to the rector of the Seminary, who in regard to the confessions of the students shall observe the spirit of canon 518, § 2, of the Code of Canon Law.

Outline of the Annual Report of the Regional Seminary of ..................................................

For the scholastic year ..................................

(to be sent to the Sacred Congregation for the Propagation of the Faith before 31 December of each year.)

1. A list of the names of all the officials and professors of the seminary.

2. The number of seminarians, distinct by Vicariates and classes ..................................................
Number of seminarians who entered this year..........
Number of students who have left because they have been ordained ...................... (add a brief note concerning the qualities of each).
Number of students who have left during the year because of other causes ............ who have been expelled ............ (give the reason why each has been expelled).

3. Number of students who have passed the examinations ......................... Number of students

who have failed in the examinations ....................
(remarks, if any).

4. Economic report:
   a) Income, itemized.
   b) Expenditures, itemized.

(Indicate the average sum spent on each student).

5. Comments regarding:
   a) The spiritual and disciplinary status of the seminary
   b) Studies
   c) Hygiene
   d) Finances
   e) Miscellaneous.

Date ........................................
Signatures of each Ordinary and of the rector of the Seminary.

This enclosure with the *Normae* of 1934 brings to a close the report on the legislation for the administration of regional seminaries subject to the Sacred Congregation for the Propagation of the Faith in China. Before going on to the commentary on the individual provisions of these *Normae*, one may very usefully review the history of each seminary in China which is considered regional and governed by the special norms of the Holy See. The establishment of 15 regional seminaries in China will therefore be considered in the following article.

## Article 3. The Constitution of 15 Regional Seminaries Subject to the Sacred Congregation for the Propagation of the Faith

### 1. *Regional Seminary of Sui-yüan*

The Regional Seminary of Sui-yüan was erected in 1936. On October 3, 1935, the Vicars Apostolic of Sui-yüan, Chi-ning (Tsining), Hsi-wan-tzu (Siwantze) and Ta-t'ung (the Vicars Apostolic of Ning-hsia and of Je-ho [Jehol] being legitimately absent), sent to the Sacred Congregation for the Propagation of the Faith the annual report of the Regional Seminary of Ta-t'ung. With this report they also called attention to the fact that "in the meeting of the Ordinaries of these regions, held in the beginning of January 1935, it was agreed, with the approval of the Apostolic Delegate, to erect a separate regional seminary for the study of philosophy, the city of Sui-yüan being designated as the best location. . . . Since the Apostolic Delegate has again approved this decree, and the General Council of the Congregation of the Immaculate Heart of Mary (of Scheut) has consented to it, the work of construction was begun in the month of March. . . . If it please God, beginning with the scholastic year 1936-1937 the theologians shall go to the Regional Seminary of Ta-t'ung, and the students in philosophy to the Regional Seminary of Sui-yüan, which shall also be conducted by the Scheut Fathers. . . ." The course of philosophy was to last for three years, and included also the more advanced courses in Chinese, Latin, English and the natural sciences.[18]

Fr. Louis Morel, C.I.C.M. de Scheut, was proposed by his superiors for the office of rector. He was appointed rector of the Regional Seminary of Sui-yüan by the Sacred Congregation on Sept. 19, 1936. On the same day the professors and the other superiors were confirmed by the Congregation.[19]

The seminary was opened on September 1, 1936. As is evident, the missions mentioned above send their students in philosophy to the Seminary of Sui-yüan: from the Province of Mongolia—the Archdiocese of Sui-yüan, the Dioceses of Ning-hsia, Hsi-wan-tzu (Siwantze) and Chi-ning (Tsining); from the Province of Manchuria—the Diocese of Je-ho (Jehol); from the Province of Shan-hsi—the Diocese of Ta-t'ung. Of these missions, Chi-ning is entrusted to the native secular clergy, the others to the Fathers of Scheut.[20]

[18] "Relatio Annua Sem. Reg. de Tatung, pro anno 1934-1935," 3 oct. 1935—*Archivum S. C. P. F.*, Ta-t'ung, a. 1935.

[19] S. C. P. F., epistola, 19 sept. 1936—*Archivum S. C. P. F.*, Sui-yüan, a. 1936.

[20] Historical notes on this seminary may be found in: Leyssen, *Formatio Cleri in Mongolia* (Pekini: Impr. des Lazaristes, 1940).

### 2. *Regional Seminary of Hsin-ching*

The seminary is situated in the city of Hsin-ching (Hsin-king, alternate name Ch'ang-ch'un), Diocese of Chi-lin (Kirin). The archives of the Sacred Congregation of the Propagation of the Faith do not reveal any document of erection of the seminary or of the canonical appointment of the rector. However, there is no doubt that the Seminary of St. Augustine is a true regional seminary. In a letter dated September 28, 1935, and sent to the Cardinal Prefect of the Sacred Congregation, Bishop Augustus Gaspais, M.E.P., the Vicar Apostolic of Chi-lin (Kirin), stated: "As I had reported to Your Eminence at the time of my visit to Rome, the Augustinian Fathers of the Assumption have accepted the administration of a major seminary for the various missions of Mandchoukuo [Man-chou-kuo], and have also agreed to the foundation of a school at Hsinking."[21]

In a letter of September 20, 1937, the same Vicar Apostolic wrote: "At Hsinking, after long and complicated negotiations, we received authorization to begin work on the construction of the regional major seminary. It may be ready to function by October of next year, under the direction of the Assumptionist Fathers. Meanwhile the latter continue to prepare themselves for the work which led them to Mandchuria [Manchuria]: the training of our native clergy."[22]

Many of the Ordinaries of Manchuria were present in Chi-lin on November 15, 1939, for the consecration of Bishop Charles Lemaire, M.E.P., co-adjutor of Chi-lin. On November 24th, Bishop Gaspais made mention of the consecration which took place on the 15th of November and added: ". . . I took the opportunity to hold a meeting of the Ordinaries of Mandchoukuo on the next day. The draft of the Rules of the Regional Seminary was studied in common, and shall now be submitted to your Most Reverend Eminence for approval. All the Ordinaries present were unanimous in their desire to have the courses start at the beginning of the year

[21] *Archivum S. C. P. F.*, Chi-lin, a. 1935.
[22] *Archivum S. C. P. F.*, Chi-lin, a. 1937.

1940 and agreed to do all that is possible to satisfy the requests of the Reverend Assumptionist Fathers and thus facilitate their work."[23] The "Draft of the Statutes and Rules of the Regional Seminary of Hsinking" was sent in to the Sacred Congregation and, after a few changes, was approved on March 30, 1940.[24]

In a letter of April 7, 1940, Bishop Gaspais could finally write: "I have the pleasure to inform Your Most Reverend Eminence that the Regional Seminary of Hsinking is at long last ready to receive the seminarians of Mandchoukuo. Yesterday, April 6th, the new building was blessed, and on the tenth of this month 53 students of philosophy and theology are to be admitted."[25]

The course of studies is of two years in philosophy and four years in theology. The seminarians of nine dioceses and prefectures of Manchuria (or Man-chou-kuo) go to this seminary, the Diocese of Je-ho (Jehol) sending its students to the Regional Seminary of Sui-yüan for philosophy and to the Regional Seminary of Ta-t'ung for theology.[26]

### 3. *The Regional Seminary of Süan-hua*

The Regional Seminary of Süan-hua (Süanhwa) is entrusted to the native secular clergy and is administered according to the Regulations of 1921. It was erected by letters of the Sacred Congregation of the Propagation of the Faith on May 9, 1932, and has a two-year course in philosophy and

[23] *Archivum S. C. P. F.*, Chi-lin, a. 1939.

[24] S. C. P. F., epistola, 30 mart. 1940—*Archivum S. C. P. F.*, Chi-lin, a. 1940.

[25] *Archivum S. C. P. F.*, Chi-lin, a. 1940.

[26] *Annuaire des Missions Catholiques de Chine* (Shanghai: Imprimerie de T'ou-sè-wè, près Zi-ka-wei), 1947, p. 26 (hereafter cited *Annuaire*). The writer has tried to give the ordinary status of the seminaries. Because of extraordinary circumstances, many changes have occurred during the past years. Thus students from seminaries closed down because of war conditions and persecution were sent to other seminaries which could still function. This fact must be kept in mind when one consults such annual publications as the *Annuaire*.

a four-year course in theology.[27] The Reverend Nicholas Wenders, a secular priest incardinated in the Vicariate Apostolic of Süan-hua, but formerly of Belgium and a member of the Society of Auxiliary Priests of the Missions, was appointed rector of the seminary in the following decree.

Decree

> The Sacred Congregation for the Propagation of the Faith, according to the wishes of their Excellencies the Vicar Apostolic of Suan-hwa-fu, the Vicar Apostolic of Fenyang, and of the Mission Superior of Yihsien, appoints Reverend Nicholas Wenders, a secular priest of the Vicariate of Suan-hwa-fu, the rector of the Regional Seminary of the same Vicariate Apostolic of Suan-hwa-fu, with all the rights and duties attached to the office. Given at Rome from the Offices of the Sacred Congregation for the Propagation of the Faith, 15 Sept. 1932.[28]

The students attending this seminary are those coming from the Diocese of Süan-hua and the Prefecture Apostolic of I-hsien (Yihsien) in the Province of Ho-pei (Hopeh), and from the Diocese of Fen-yang and the Prefecture Apostolic of Hung-tung in the Province of Shan-hsi.[29]

### 4. *Regional Seminary of Cha-la*

The Regional Seminary of Cha-la is located in the village of Cha-la near Pei-ching (Peking), and was erected in 1934. The Ordinaries of Pei-ching, An-kuo (Ankwo), Cheng-ting, Shun-te (Shunteh), T'ien-chin (Tientsin) and Yung-p'ing (all Lazarists) petitioned their Superior General in a letter of January 19, 1934, to obtain for the major seminary of Cha-la recognition as a regional seminary. The seminary was to be the regional seminary for the above mentioned missions of the Lazarists and for the missions of Pao-ting and Chao-hsien of the secular clergy. The major seminary

[27] S. C. P. F., epistola, 9 maii 1932—*Archivum S. C. P. F.*, Süan-hua, a. 1932.

[28] *Archivum S. C. P. F.*, Süan-hua, a. 1932.

[29] *Annuaire*, 1947, pp. 26-27.

had been functioning well since 1921, and now (in 1934) wished to become in fact a true regional seminary.[30]

The Sacred Congregation, therefore, on July 24, 1934, recognized this seminary as a true regional seminary, entrusted it to the Congregation of the Mission (Lazarists) to be ruled in accordance with the Regulations of 1934. The Reverend Octave Ferreux, C.M., was appointed the first rector, and the other superiors and professors were approved.[31] As indicated above, the Regional Seminary of Chala receives students in philosophy and theology from the Archdiocese of Pei-ching, and the Dioceses of An-kuo, Cheng-ting, Shun-te, T'ien-chin, Yung-p'ing, Chao-hsien and Pao-ting.

### 5. *Regional Seminary of Ching-hsien*

On October 31, 1940, the Vicars Apostolic of Hsien-hsien (Sienhsien) and Yung-nien, and the Prefects Apostolic of Ta-ming and Ching-hsien (Kinghsien) sent to the Sacred Congregation a petition to have the Seminary of Ching-hsien constituted a regional seminary subject to the Regulations of 1934. This petition and the rules of discipline for the seminary were forwarded to the Sacred Congregation by the Apostolic Delegate, Archbishop Mario Zanin, on January 9, 1941.[32] After the Society of Jesus had agreed to accept the administration of the seminary, the Sacred Congregation for the Propagation of the Faith erected the seminary as a true regional seminary, entrusted it to the Jesuits, and appointed the Very Reverend Leopold Brellinger, S.J., the Prefect Apostolic of Ching-hsien, as the first rector. The other professors and superiors were likewise approved, and the rules of the seminary were confirmed for a period of seven years.[33]

[30] *Archivum S. C. P. F.*, Pei-ching, a. 1934.

[31] S. C. P. F., epistola, 24 iul. 1934—*Archivum S. C. P. F.*, Pei-chung, a. 1924.

[32] *Archivum S. C. P. F.*, Ching-hsien, a. 1941.

[33] S. C. P. F., epistola, 17 mart. 1941—*Archivum S. C. P. F.*, Ching-hsien, a. 1941.

The seminary receives students from the Dioceses of Ching-hsien, Hsien-hsien, Ta-ming (all Jesuit missions) and Yung-nien (secular clergy) in the Province of Ho-pei (Hopeh), and from the Diocese of Hsü-chou (Süchow) in the Province of Chiang-su (Kiangsu).[34]

### 6. *Regional Seminary of Chi-nan*

This seminary, built in 1924, is situated in the village of Hung-chia-lou near the city of Chi-nan (Tsinan). It was the major seminary for the mission of Chi-nan and for several other missions of the Province of Shan-tung. After the Norms of 1934 were published, the Sacred Congregation expressed its wish, through the Apostolic Delegate, that this seminary become a true regional seminary.[35] In October of 1934 the Ordinaries of Chi-nan, Chih-fou (Chefoo), Chou-ts'un (Chowtsun), I-tu-hsien (Iduhsien), Wei-hai-wei and Lin-ch'ing (Lintsing) requested of the Minister General of the Order of Friars Minor that his Order undertake the administration of the regional seminary according to the norms of the Holy See. After many difficulties were overcome, the Sacred Congregation instructed the Apostolic Delegate in China to consult with the Ordinaries concerned, and to see to it that everything was arranged so that the major seminary of Chi-nan could be opened as a true regional seminary at the beginning of the scholastic year 1936-1937.[36]

This letter of the Congregation must be considered as the document of the erection, since no other decree nor any other document concerning this matter can be found in the archives of the Congregation. The Rules of the seminary were approved in a letter of June 12, 1936,[37] and "according to the Norms for Regional Seminaries committed to Religious In-

[34] *Annuaire*, 1947, pp. 26-27.

[35] S. C. P. F., epistola, 25 maii 1934—*Archivum S. C. P. F.*, Chi-nan, a. 1934.

[36] S. C. P. F., epistola, 8 apr. 1936—*Archivum S. C. P. F.*, Chi-nan, a. 1936.

[37] S. C. P. F., epistola, 12 iun. 1936—*Archivum S. C. P. F.*, Chi-nan, a. 1936.

stitutes" the Reverend Hyacinth Wilmes, O.F.M., was appointed the "Rector of the Regional Seminary of St. John the Baptist in Tsinan-Hungkialou" on November 11, 1936.[38]

This seminary receives students from the Archdiocese of Chi-nan, the Dioceses of Chou-ts'un and Chih-fou, and the Prefectures Apostolic of I-tu-hsien, Wei-hai-wei and Lin-ch'ing—all of the Province of Shan-tung.[39]

### 7. *Regional Seminary of Ta-t'ung*

The Regional Seminary of Ta-t'ung was the first to be erected under the new law of the Code. Its constitution gave rise to the Norms of 1921. Historically it is of prime importance. The Vicars Apostolic of Central Mongolia, Southwest Mongolia, North Kan-su, and the Prefect Apostolic of South Kan-su (in the name also of the Vicar Apostolic of East Mongolia),[40] met with the Very Reverend Joseph Rutten, Superior General of Scheut, on February 1, 1921, and sent the following letter to the Cardinal Prefect of the Sacred Congregation for the Propagation of the Faith:

> Siwantze, 1 Feb. 1921.
>
> Most Reverend Eminence,
>
> The undersigned Ordinaries of the Scheut Missions in China, convened at Siwantze with the Very Reverend Father Rutten, Superior of Scheut, complying with the desire which the Very Reverend Father General has communicated to them on the part of Your Eminence, . . . have agreed to establish a central seminary for the students of their respective missions.
>
> The city of Tatung having been chosen as the site, and the local Ordinary having agreed to make available a building next to a church for the provisional establishment of the seminary, it has been decided that the seminary will be erected there, with a start made in August, 1921. . . .

[38] S. C. P. F., epistola, 11 nov. 1936—*Archivum S. C. P. F.*, Chi-nan, a. 1936.

[39] *Annuaire*, 1947, p. 26.

[40] The missions today are: Hsi-wan-tzu (Siwantze), Sui-yüan, Lan-chou, Ch'in-chou (Tsinchow), Je-ho respectively.

> Your Eminence will find enclosed the general statutes which the same Ordinaries have compiled in view of the organization and administration of the planned seminary, as well as the program of studies. . . .[41]

The Sacred Congregation approved the Central Seminary of Ta-t'ung for the missions entrusted to the Scheut Fathers and appointed the Very Reverend Constantine Daems as the first rector.[42] In the month of March, 1921, the Sacred Congregation drew up the "Norms for Regional Seminaries in China" and sent them to the Central Seminary of Ta-t'ung. It is certain that in the creation of these norms the Congregation used the general statutes sent in for approval by the Ordinaries of Scheut for the administration of the Central Seminary of Ta-t'ung. The *Projet d'Organisation et d'Administration du Seminaire Central de Tatung* should be considered one of the fundamental sources of the two sets of norms made by the Congregation in 1921 and 1934. Many particular provisions of the general statutes were changed however by the Sacred Congregation.[43]

In 1924 the seminary moved into its new buildings outside the city of Ta-t'ung. In 1930 the first rector, Fr. Daems, was elected Superior General of Scheut, and Fr. James Leyssen, C.I.C.M., was appointed as the new rector.[44] The seminary was officially committed to the Scheut Fathers in 1935 and subjected to the new norms of 1934, so that many of the rights and duties which earlier were proper to the Ordinaries of the region, now (in 1935) devolved upon the religious institute of Scheut.[45]

From the beginning of the scholastic year 1936-1937 the

[41] *Archivum S. C. P. F.*, Sinae—Negotia Communia, a. 1921.

[42] S. C. P. F., epistola, 21 iun. 1921—*Archivum S. C. P. F.*, Sinae—Negotia Communia, a. 1921.

[43] See the text of these general statutes in Part III (Documents), Document 2.

[44] S. C. P. F., decr., 22 sept. 1930—*Archivum S. C. P. F.*, Ta-t'ung, a. 1930.

[45] S. C. P. F., epistola, 11 ian. 1935—*Archivum S. C. P. F.*, Ta-t'ung, a. 1935.

Regional Seminary of Ta-t'ung became a school of theology only, the students in philosophy being sent to the newly erected philosophical Regional Seminary of Sui-yüan. The missions which send their students to the Seminary of Ta-t'ung are: the Archdiocese of Sui-yüan, the Dioceses of Ning-hsia, Hsi-wan-tzu (Siwantze) and Chi-ning (Tsining) of the Province of Mongolia; the Diocese of Je-ho of the Province of Manchuria; and the Diocese of Ta-t'ung of the Province of Shan-hsi.[46]

### 8. *The Regional Seminary of T'ai-yüan*[47]

The Vicars Apostolic of T'ai-yüan, Lu-an and Shou-chou (Shohchow) and the Prefect Apostolic of Yü-tz'u (Yütze), all Franciscans, sent a petition to the Sacred Congregation for the Propagation of the Faith on September 14, 1934, through the ministry of the General of their Order. A large building had been erected by the Vicar Apostolic of T'ai-yüan to receive the major seminarians of these four missions, and thus there resulted the above mentioned Ordinaries' request that this seminary be constituted as the Regional Seminary of T'ai-yüan, subject to the special norms of the Sacred Congregation.[48]

After the Minister General of the Franciscans had agreed to take over the administration of the seminary, the Sacred Congregation recognized it as a regional seminary that was to be ruled according to the Norms of 1934. The letter of erection also stated that this seminary was to serve all the missions of Shan-hsi, so that the missions of Fen-yang and Hung-tung could send their students to this seminary if they

[46] *Annuaire*, 1947, pp. 26-27. Note that the *Annuaire* uses names of provinces, missions, alternate and modern names of cities, etc., to designate the location of one and the same seminary. For example, in the *Annuaire*, 1947, pp. 26-29, the names "Howho, Kweisui, Suiyüan" are used in designation of the Regional Seminary of Sui-yüan.

[47] Modern name: Yang-ch'ü.

[48] *Archivum S. C. P. F.*, T'ai-yüan, a. 1934.

so desired.[49] A letter of July 27, 1936, appointed Fr. Elias Carosi, O.F.M., the rector of the Seminary, and confirmed the appointments of the other superiors and professors.[50]

The seminary began with a program of studies which called for a three-year course of philosophy and a four-year course of theology. It served the Archdiocese of T'ai-yüan, the Dioceses of Lu-an, Shou-chou (Shohchow) and Yü-tz'u, and the Prefecture Apostolic of Chiang-chou (Kiangchow) —all of the province of Shan-hsi.[51] From its very foundation it also served the Franciscan Missions and the secular clergy missions of the Province of Shen-hsi.[52] Of this Province, the following missions send their students to the Regional Seminary of T'ai-yüan: the Archdiocese of Hsi-an (Sian), the Dioceses of Feng-hsiang (Fengsiang), San-yüan, Yen-an, and the Prefectures Apostolic of T'ung-chou (Tung-chow) and Chou-chih (Chowchih).[53]

### 9. *Regional Seminary of Lan-chou*[54]

Only little information seems obtainable concerning the Seminary of Lan-chou (Lanchow), which is however regarded as a true regional seminary. The Vicar Apostolic of Ch'in-chou (Tsinchow), writing for the Ordinaries of the region of Kan-su on January 31, 1938, petitioned the Sacred Congregation for the Propagation of the Faith for canonical recognition of the regional seminary. On December 22, 1938, the Superior General of the Society of the Divine Word re-

[49] S. C. P. F., epistola, 11 ian. 1935—*Archivum S. C. P. F.*, T'ai-yüan, a. 1935.

[50] S. C. P. F., epistola, 27 iul. 1936—*Archivum S. C. P. F.*, T'ai-yüan, a. 1936.

[51] *Annuaire*, 1947, p. 27.

[52] Shen-hsi: the spelling of the Chinese sound is the same as for "Shansi" and should therefore be Shan-hsi. However, in order to avoid confusion, the writer will render it Shen-hsi. Shen-hsi is therefore used for Shensi, and Shan-hsi for Shansi.

[53] Cf. *Annuaire*, 1939-1941; S. de Nardis, *Il Seminario Regionale Giovanni da Montecorvino nel suo Terzo Anniversario* (Taiyuanfu: Typis Missionis Catholicae, 1939), p. 21.

[54] Modern name: Kao-lan.

sponded to the invitation of the Congregation and reported that his Society was ready to assume the administration of the Regional Seminary of Lan-chou.[55]

Because of the wars that followed and the remoteness of the region, no other official documents are available. The seminary did begin to function as a regional seminary in 1938, and was under the direction of the Society of the Divine Word. There is no formal decree of erection nor any record of approval of the rules etc.; yet, inasmuch as the seminary was offered to the Society of the Divine Word by the Sacred Congregation, and was accepted by that Society, one may regard this as the equivalent of a general approbation. Since the complete organization of the seminary as a regional seminary was hindered by circumstances beyond the control of the missioners and the Society, this general approbation suggests that it be considered a regional seminary, even though not all the provisions of law could be carried out in its constitution. For this reason the writer has included the Seminary of Lan-chou in the list of regional seminaries.

This seminary serves the missions of the Ecclesiastical Province of Kan-su, which embraces the three civil provinces of Kan-su, Hsin-chiang (Sinkiang) and Ch'ing-hai (Tsinghai or Kokonor).[56]

### 10. *Regional Seminary of Shang-hai*

In June of 1947 the Ordinaries of the Province of Chiang-su (Kiangsu) petitioned the Sacred Congregation for the Propagation of the Faith to recognize as the regional seminary for the Province of Chiang-su the major seminary of the Diocese of Shang-hai, which seminary is located at Hsü-chia-hui (Zi-ka-wei). In November of the same year the General of the Society of Jesus agreed to assume the administration of the seminary. Up to that time the seminary had been administered by the Jesuits, but as a diocesan, and not

[55] *Archivum S. C. P. F.*, Lan-chou, a. 1938.

[56] *Annuaire*, 1947, p. 27; *Les Missions de Chine* (Shanghai: Procure des Lazaristes, 1942), pp. 188-201 (hereafter cited *Les Missions*).

as a regional seminary. By its decree of November 7, 1947, the Sacred Congregation erected the Regional Seminary of Shang-hai, at Hsü-chia-hui (Zi-ka-wei), placed it under the administration of the Jesuits to be ruled according to the Norms of 1934, and declared it to be the regional seminary for the Province of Chiang-su (Kiangsu).[57]

Although the seminary was erected for the entire Province of Chiang-su, nevertheless by special permission of the Sacred Congregation, the Diocese of Hsü-chou (Süchow) sends its students to the Regional Seminary of Ching-hsien (King-hsien). The Regional Seminary of Shang-hai began to operate in 1947-1948, and receives students from the Dioceses of Shang-hai and Hai-men, as well as from the Archdiocese of Nan-ching.[58]

### 11. *Regional Seminary of Wu-hu*

The Regional Seminary of Wu-hu is located in the city of Süan-ch'eng in the Diocese of Wu-hu. In a letter of March 22, 1947, His Excellency Archbishop Mario Zanin, Apostolic Delegate to China, approved the proposal of the Ordinaries of the Province of An-hui (Anhwei) that the major seminary of the Diocese of Wu-hu be constituted a regional seminary for the Archdiocese of An-ching (Anking), the Dioceses of Pang-fou (Pengpu) and Wu-hu, and the Prefecture Apostolic of T'un-ch'i (Tunki). The Sacred Congregation was likewise informed in the same letter that the Vicar Apostolic of Nan-ching (Nanking) sought permission to send his students to Wu-hu because the language as spoken in his mission was more akin to that which was spoken and used in An-hui, and differed from the language as used by the inhabitants of Shang-hai. The Apostolic Delegate therefore suggested that the Major Seminary of Wu-hu be constituted as a regional seminary.[59]

The Regional Seminary of Wu-hu was erected by the Sac-

[57] S. C. P. F., decr., 7 nov. 1947—*Archivum S. C. P. F.*, Shang-hai, a. 1947.

[58] *Annuaire*, 1947, p. 27.

[59] *Archivum S. C. P. F.*, Wu-hu a. 1947.

red Congregation on June 13, 1947, and entrusted to the care of the Jesuits according to the Norms of 1934.[60] It is frequented by the students of the four Churches of the Ecclesiastical Province of An-hui, and before 1948 was attended also by the students of the Archdiocese of Nan-ching (Nanking).[61]

### 12. *Regional Seminary of K'ai-feng*

The Regional Seminary of K'ai-feng was officially opened in September, 1932. It was entrusted to the Pontifical Institute of Milan for the Foreign Missions by letters of the Sacred Congregation for the Propagation of the Faith on Sept. 26, 1931, and its rules of discipline were approved on December 7, 1932. Reverend Aloysius Nogara was appointed the rector, the other superiors and professors also being confirmed by the Congregation in a letter of April 22, 1932.[62]

The courses of study embrace a three-year course in philosophy and a four-year course in sacred theology. All but two of the nine missions of the Province of Ho-nan send their seminarians to this seminary. The two Society of the Divine Word missions, namely the Diocese of Hsin-yang (Sinyang) and the Prefecture Apostolic of Hsin-hsiang (Sinsiang) send their students to the intermission seminary of Yen-chou (Yenchow) in the Province of Shan-tung. Before the activities of the Communists, the Diocese of Han-chung and the Prefecture Apostolic of Hsing-an (Hingan) of the Province of Shen-hsi also sent their students to the Regional Seminary of K'ai-feng.[63]

### 13. *Regional Seminary of Han-k'ou*

The Regional Seminary of St. Bonaventure was erected as a central seminary for the regions of Hu-pei (Hupeh) and Hu-nan in 1921. At that time all the missions of both regions were entrusted to the Order of Friars Minor with

[60] S. C. P. F., decr., 13 iun. 1947—*Archivum S. C. P. F.*, Wu-hu, a. 1947.

[61] Cf. the *Annuaire*, 1942-1949.

[62] *Archivum S. C. P. F.*, K'ai-feng, a. 1931-1932.

[63] *Annuaire*, 1934-1947.

the exception of the Vicariate Apostolic of North Hu-nan. This latter mission was served by the Order of Hermits of St. Augustine. In the course of time it was broken down into the present Dioceses of Ch'ang-te (Changteh) and Yüan-ling, and the Prefectures Apostolic of Li-chou (Lichow) and Yo-chou (Yochow). The central seminary was first located in the city of Wu-ch'ang, was later moved to Ching-chou, modern Chiang-ling (Kingchow—Kiangling), and finally to Han-k'ou (Hankow) where it remained. The seminary was vigorously promoted by some of China's great apostles in modern times, namely Bishops John Mondaini, Gratian Gennaro, Hermenegild Ricci, Modestus Everaerts, Natalis Gubbels, Trudo Jans, and Eugene Massi. Several of these apostolic men suffered martyrdom during the past few decades.[64]

In the summer of 1930 ten Vicars and Prefects Apostolic of the regions of Hu-pei and Hu-nan sent petitions to the Sacred Congregation for the Propagation of the Faith to the effect that this seminary be constituted a regional seminary, entrusted to the Franciscans according to the Regulations of the Sacred Congregation for regional seminaries. These Ordinaries represented missions of the Franciscans, of the Hermits of St. Augustine, of the Passionists, and of the Chinese secular clergy. The petitions of these Superiors were presented to the Congregation *in globo* by the Minister General of the Friars Minor on February 27, 1931. The rules of discipline, the program of studies, the scholastic *horarium* and a list of the textbooks were likewise submitted for approval. Reverend Clementine Van der Borght was presented for the office of rector, and the names of the other superiors and professors were submitted for confirmation.[65] These various documents were all approved by the Sacred Congregation, and Fr. Borght was named as rector.[66] Fr. Van der

[64] For a résume of the early history confer *Apostolicum—Periodicum Pastorale et Asceticum pro Missionibus*, III (1932), 440 ss.

[65] *Archivum S. C. P. F.*, Han-k'ou, a. 1931.

[66] S. C. P. F., epistola, 18 ian. 1932—*Archivum S. C. P. F.*, Han-k'ou, a. 1932.

Borght, however, never took possession of his office, and accordingly Fr. Mansuetus Maggini, O.F.M., was nominated and appointed rector in 1933.[67]

The rules of discipline were examined and approved, both by a special commission in China consisting of the Apostolic Delegate and two competent priests, and also by the Sacred Congregation in Rome, and were then published in the *Collectanea Commissionis Synodalis* to serve as an exemplar for the rules of other regional seminaries and of all major seminaries in general.[68]

Until 1938 all the missions of the two Provinces of Hu-pei and Hu-nan sent their students to the Regional Seminary of Han-k'ou, but since that time some missions have sent their students to other seminaries. However, even after 1938 the majority of the clerics were still sent to Han-k'ou.[69]

### 14. *Regional Seminary of Fu-chien*

The Regional Seminary of Fu-chien (Fukien) was erected by the Sacred Congregation for the Propagation of the Faith for the Province of Fu-chien in 1936, and entrusted to the Order of Preachers.[70] Fr. Hilary Albers, O.P., was appointed the first rector of the institution.[71]

The program of studies of the seminary provides for a year of study preparatory to the study of philosophy. During this year as well as during the two-year course of philosophy, classes are held in mathematics, chemistry, physics, biology, anthropology, and Chinese language and literature. The courses in Chinese are continued during the study of theology because of the special difficulty of the language. Introduction to philosophy and logic are taught already in

[67] S. C. P. F., epistola 12 iul. 1933—*Archivum S. C. P. F.*, Han-k'ou, a. 1933.

[68] *Coll. Comm. Syn.*, V (1932), 736-744.

[69] Cf. the *Annuaire*, 1932-1947.

[70] S. C. P. F., epistola, 20 iun. 1936—*Archivum S. C. P. F.*, Fu-chou, a. 1936.

[71] S. C. P. F., epistola, 5 sept. 1936—*Archivum S. C. P. F.*, Fu-chou, a. 1936.

the second semester of the preparatory year. The *ratio studiorum* also calls for a fifth year of theology to be introduced if possible. This year would be placed after the course in philosophy, but before the regular course in theology. The year would be used for the study of fundamental theology, apologetics and other preparatory subjects.[72]

The Regional Seminary of Fu-chien serves the Archdiocese of Fu-chou, the Dioceses of Hsia-men (Amoy), Fu-ning (Fu-ning) and Ting-chou (Tingchow), and the Prefectures of Chien-ou (Kienow) and Shao-wu.[73]

### 15. *Regional Seminary of Hsiang-kang*

The Regional Seminary of Hsiang-kang (Hongkong) is located on the in-shore island and harbor of Aberdeen,[74] Hsiang-kang. The Sacred Congregation for the Propagation of the Faith offered the administration of this seminary to the Society of Jesus in a letter of December 4, 1926. At that time the seminary was being constructed. The General of the Jesuits responded in the affirmative on December 15, 1926, and the Sacred Congregation informed the Apostolic Delegate in China of these matters in a letter of January 20, 1927.[75]

On February 22, 1927, six Ordinaries of the region of Kuang-tung (Kwangtung), namely the Vicars Apostolic of Kuang-chou (Canton), Hsiang-kang (Hongkong), Pei-hai (Pakhoi), the Vicar Delegate of Shao-chou (Shiuchow), the Bishop of Macau,[76] and the Prefect Apostolic of Chiang-men (Kongmoon) entered upon the following agreement in a meeting at Hsiang-kang:

1. A regional seminary is to be erected at Hsiang-kang (Hongkong).

[72] "Ratio Studiorum Seminarii Regionalis de Fukien," art. 2, 3—*Archivum S.C.P.F.*, Fu-chou, a. 1937.

[73] *Annuaire*, 1947, p. 28.

[74] Called Hsiang-kang-tzu by the Chinese.

[75] *Archivum S.C.P.F.*, Hsiang-kang, a. 1926-1927.

[76] Official Portuguese: Macau; Chinese name: Ao-men; often written in English as Macao.

2. The Jesuits shall have the administration of the seminary according to the norms to be given by the Sacred Congregation for the Propagation of the Faith.
3. Each Vicar Apostolic shall pay for the expenses of the students he sends to the seminary.
4. The Vicars Apostolic thank the Pontifical Work of St. Peter for its charity, and shall, as agreed, pay for the period of 20 years an interest of 2½% on the debt. The funds borrowed are being used for the construction of the seminary and for its furnishings.
5. The ownership of the regional seminary belongs to the Sacred Congregation for the Propagation of the Faith, the use to the Vicars Apostolic. The legal representative before the civil government shall be the Vicar Apostolic of Hsiang-kang, or by his delegation the rector of the seminary. No radical changes nor alienation of property may be made until the Sacred Congregation has been consulted in the matter.
6. Missions to be erected in South China, whether entrusted to the foreign or to the native clergy, shall have the right to send their students to this seminary.
7. The house is to be entrusted to the Fathers of the Society of Jesus. The rector of the seminary shall see to it that he observes all the provisions of this agreement.[77]

Some points of special interest appear in this agreement. First of all the seminary, although erected primarily for the Province of Kuang-tung (Kwangtung), is ready also to accept students from other missions of South China. Thus before the founding of the Regional Seminary of Fu-chien the missions of the Province of Fu-chien (Fukien) sent their students to the seminary at Hsiang-kang. In fact the seminary came to be called the Regional Seminary for South China.

[77] Delegatus Apostolicus in Sinis ad S. C. P. F., rapporto, 28 febr. 1927—*Archivum S. C. P. F.*, Hsiang-kang (Hongkong), n. 1299/27 prot.

Msgr. James E. Walsh, Prefect Apostolic of Chiang-men (Kongmoon), signed the agreement also for the future missions of Maryknoll in South China. Today these missions send their students to Hsiang-kang. The Bishop of Macau also entered into this agreement. The Diocese of Macau depends not on the Sacred Congregation for the Propagation of the Faith but on the Sacred Congregation for Extraordinary Ecclesiastical Affairs. Nevertheless in this matter the Bishop of Macau made common cause with the Ordinaries of the Province of Kuang-tung despite the fact that Macau has its own major seminary.

The archives of the Sacred Congregation do not reveal any approbation of this pact as made by the Ordinaries, and in fact no other document can be found in the archives from 1927 to 1934 regarding this seminary. The agreement was observed, however, and the seminary began to function. In May, 1934, the Sacred Congregation sent the Norms of 1934 to the General of the Jesuits and requested him to enforce them in the Regional Seminary of Hsiang-kang. At the same time the Congregation asked that the rules of discipline, the program of studies, the scholastic *horarium,* and the list of textbooks be submitted for approval, and that a candidate be proposed for the office of rector. It was allowable to propose as a candidate the very person who then was holding the office of rector.[78] After these documents were submitted, the Sacred Congregation approved the program of studies, the textbooks, etc., and appointed Fr. Thomas Cooney, S.J., as the rector. The other professors and superiors were likewise confirmed.[79] The rules of discipline were confirmed and approved on April 8, 1935.[80]

Thus for the Regional Seminary of Hsiang-kang (Hongkong), as well as for several others, although there is no

[78] S. C. P. F., epistola, 26 maii 1934—*Archivum S. C. P. F.*, Hsiang-kang, a. 1934.

[79] S. C. P. F., epistola, 11 ian. 1935—*Archivum S. C. P. F.*, Hsiang-kang, a. 1935.

[80] S. C. P. F., epistola, 8 apr. 1935—*Archivum S. C. P. F.*, Hsiang-kang, a. 1935.

formal document of erection, nevertheless an equivalent erection is easily proved. The letter of the Sacred Congregation issued on December 4, 1926, to the Superior General of the Jesuits and offering the administration of the seminary to the Society; the General's affirmative response; the letter of May 26, 1934, imposing the Norms of 1934 on the seminary; the letters of January 11, and April 8, 1935, approving the studies, acknowledging the rules, appointing the rector, etc.—all these definitely prove the express intervention of the Holy See with regard to the major seminary at Hsiang-kang. This seminary must therefore be considered a true regional seminary. For the rest, it is so considered in China, and thus regarded also by the Sacred Congregation for the Propagation of the Faith.

This seminary receives students from the missions of the Province of Kuang-tung (Kwangtung) and from the two Maryknoll Missions (Wu-chou [Wuchow] and Kuei-lin [Kweilin]) in the Province of Kuang-hsi (Kwangsi). However, in the Province of Kuang-tung, the Diocese of Pei-hai (Pakhoi) and Shan-t'ou (Swatow), entrusted to the Paris Foreign Mission Society, have been sending their students to the seminary of their Society located and Penang, Malacca.[81] Finally, the Diocese of Macau has its own major seminary.[82]

## Appendix

### Intermissional Seminaries

Besides the regional seminaries that have been treated here, and the major diocesan seminaries which several of the dioceses have established, there are also other seminaries called central, common, or intermissional. These intermissional or interdiocesan seminaries are entrusted to some missionary or religious institute usually by the authority of the Vicars Apostolic concerned and they receive students from missions of their institute, not however exclusively. Since these seminaries are not recognized as regional by the

[81] Cf. the *Annuaire*, 1940-1948.

[82] Cf., v. g., *Les Missions*, 1942, p. 422.

Sacred Congregation for the Propagation of the Faith, and do not observe the special norms edited by the Congregation, they cannot be called regional in the juridic sense of the word.

The Apostolic Constitution *Quotidie Nos,* April 11, 1946, makes mention of 12 regional seminaries in China (Sui-yüan and Ta-t'ung forming one seminary in this reckoning) and 5 intermissional seminaries.[83] In the meantime the Seminaries of Wu-hu and of Shang-hai have been canonically erected as regional seminaries, so that three intermissional seminaries remain.

### 1. *Intermissional Seminary of Yen-chou*[84]

The seminary is located in the town of Tai-chia-chuang in the Diocese of Yen-chou (Yenchow) in Shan-tung province. It receives the major seminarians of the Dioceses of Yen-chou, I-chou (Ichow), Ts'ao-chou (Tsaochow), Ch'ing-tao (Tsingtao), missions of the Society of the Divine Word, and Yang-ku, which is in the care of the native secular clergy.[85] These missions are all in Shan-tung province. From the Ecclesiastical Province of Ho-nan, the Diocese of Hsin-yang (Sinyang) and the Prefecture of Hsin-hsiang (Sin-siang), both missions of the Society of the Divine Word, send their students to this seminary at Yen-chou.[86] The administration of the seminary is of course entrusted to the Society of the Divine Word.

### 2. *Intermissional Seminary of Ning-po*

The seminary of Ning-po was located in the Diocese of Ning-po[87] in Che-chiang (Chekiang) province. The seminary belongs to the Congregation of the Mission and receives students from the four missions of the Province of Che-

[83] *AAS,* XXXVIII (1946), 302.
[84] Modern name: Tzu-yang.
[85] *Annuaire,* 1947, p. 26.
[86] *Annuaire,* 1941-1947.
[87] Modern name: Yin-hsien.

chiang, namely Hang-chou, T'ai-chou, Ning-po, and Li-shui.[88] As was pointed out elsewhere, the Lazarists contemplated the constitution of this seminary as a regional seminary shortly after the Apostolic Visitation of Bishop de Guébriant. However, it never became a regional seminary juridically. Just recently the seminary was moved to the city of Chia-hsing (Kashing) in the Archdiocese of Hang-chou (Hang-chow). It could well have become a regional seminary except for the present state of affairs in China.

### 3. *Intermissional Seminary of Ch'eng-tu*

This seminary is in the city of Pai-lu-ch'ang (Pehlu-chang), Diocese of Ch'eng-tu, Province of Ssu-ch'uan (Szechwan). It was founded by the Paris Foreign Mission Society for the students of missions belonging to this Society. The students of missions of the Chinese secular clergy were also to be admitted. In fact, however, not all of these missions, not even all the missions belonging to the Paris Foreign Mission Society, send their students to this seminary. In the beginning several of the missions continued to send their students to Penang, Malacca. The most recent arrangement for the Province of Ssu-ch'uan is the following:

a. Dioceses of Ch'eng-tu, Sui-fu, Chia-ting (Kiating) and Shun-ch'ing (Shunking): students go to the seminary at Ch'eng-tu.
b. Dioceses of K'ang-ting and Ning-yüan: students go to the major diocesan seminary of K'un-ming in Yün-nan province.
c. Archdiocese of Ch'ung-ch'ing (Chungking) and Diocese of Wan-hsien have their own major seminaries.[89]

Negotiations to have the seminary at Ch'ung-ch'ing constituted a regional seminary were under way, but have been interrupted by the sad conditions which prevail at present.

[88] Cf. the *Annuaire*, 1933-1948.
[89] *Annuaire*, 1941-1947.

# PART II

# CANONICAL COMMENTARY

## CHAPTER IV

## FUNDAMENTAL LAW OF THE CODE OF CANON LAW

### ARTICLE 1. DISTINCTION OF VARIOUS TYPES OF SEMINARIES

The fundamental law for regional seminaries is found in canons 1354, § 3, and 1357, § 4, of the Code of Canon Law.

> Si constitui Seminarium dioecesanum nequeat, aut in constituto Seminario conveniens institutio, praesertim in philosophicis ac theologicis disciplinis, desideretur, Episcopus alumnos in alienum Seminarium mittat, nisi Seminarium interdioecesanum vel regionale, auctoritate apostolica, constitutum fuerit.[1]
>
> Seminarii interdioecesani vel regionalis regimen universum et administratio regitur normis a Sancta Sede statutis.[2]

The commentators see in these canons a juridical distinction of seminaries into two categories; on the one hand, there are diocesan seminaries, on the other, regional, interdiocesan, common or central. Thus Coronata[3] distinguishes the diocesan seminary serving one diocese, the interdiocesan or regional seminary serving several dioceses of the same region, central seminaries serving several dioceses of the same or of several nations. According to Wernz-Vidal,[4] the seminary is diocesan when proper to an individual diocese, and it is interdiocesan, regional, or provincial when

1 Can. 1354, § 3.

2 Can. 1357, § 4.

3 *Institutiones Iuris Canonici ad Usum Utriusque Cleri et Scholarum* (2. ed., 5 vols., Taurini: Marietti, 1939-1947), II, n. 934 (hereafter cited *Institutiones*).

4 *Ius Canonicum* (7 vols. in 9, Romae: Universitas Gregoriana, 1927-1946; Vol. II, 3. ed., 1943; Vol. V, 3. ed., 1946), IV, ii, n. 688.

common to an entire ecclesiastical province; national when common to all the provinces of the same nation. The *Directorium Seminariorum*[5] defines as diocesan a seminary which educates the students of one diocese or mission; interdiocesan, central or regional, one which trains the students of several missions or dioceses. Similar distinctions are made by Vermeersch—Creusen,[6] Cappello,[7] Cracco,[8] and by practically all other authors.

The authors therefore consider interdiocesan and regional seminaries as one and the same juridical institute, to be distinguished from the diocesan seminary. If any distinction is made between the interdiocesan and the regional seminary, the distinction is factual not juridical. The interdiocesan seminary serves several missions or dioceses, the regional seminary a whole province or perhaps several provinces of the same region or even all the Churches of one or of several nations. In these latter cases the regional seminary is further divided into the common, the national and the central seminary. That these factual distinctions are purely theoretic has been demonstrated in the historical part of this dissertation, for there exist in China true regional seminaries which are also called regional seminaries whether they serve several missions of one province, all the missions of one province, all the missions of two provinces, or several missions only of three provinces.

In law, however, not the factual but the juridic distinction is of importance. According to the uniformly accepted view of the authors, when the Code of Canon Law speaks of interdiocesan or regional seminaries founded by papal authority and governed by special norms of the Holy See, one

[5] *Directorium Seminariorum in Sinis* (Pekini: Auctoribus de Scheut, 1949), n. 132 (hereafter cited *Directorium*).

[6] *Epitome,* II, n. 685.

[7] *Summa Iuris Canonici* (3 vols., Romae: Apud Aedes Universitatis Gregorianae, 1940-1945; Vols. I et II, 4. ed., 1945; Vol. III, 2. ed., 1940), II, n. 513 (hereafter cited *Summa*).

[8] *De Seminariorum Sinensium Institutione* (Shanghai: Don Bosco Industrial School Printing Press, 1946), p. 11.

is not to think of the interdiocesan and the regional seminaries as two distinct juridic institutions. On the contrary, they are one and the same, namely, seminaries which are common to several dioceses, as distinct from the seminary which is diocesan, that is, proper to one definite diocese.

## Article 2. Authority Required to Establish a Regional Seminary

Canon 1354, § 3, speaks of the interdiocesan or regional seminary established by papal authority. It is to be noted that the canon does not state that these seminaries can be erected by papal authority alone. The primary purpose of paragraph three of canon 1354 is not that of identifying the authority necessary for the constitution of the regional or interdiocesan seminary. This paragraph is primarily concerned with the proper training of ecclesiastical students of poor or undeveloped dioceses. If the Bishop cannot establish a seminary of his own, or if his established seminary is not able to give the education and training demanded by the Holy See for the formation of the clergy, then the Bishop is obliged to send his students to the seminary of another diocese where the desired education can be obtained. If, however, a regional seminary has been established by papal authority, the evident meaning of the canon is that the Bishop is not free to summarily send his students to a diocesan seminary of another diocese, but is obliged to make use of this regional seminary provided by the Holy See. This would be the general rule, although no one would deny that in a particular case the Bishop could send an individual student elsewhere. This interpretation of the canon, namely, an interpretation which puts the emphasis on the Bishop's obligation to provide for the education of his clerics, is consonant with the various papal pronouncements on regional seminaries from the Council of Trent to the Code of Canon Law.[9] A similar interpretation, putting the emphasis on the obligation of the Bishops, and not on the last phrase of para-

[9] See the historical summary of such pronouncements in the first part of this dissertation.

graph three of canon 1354, is also quite uniform and consistent in official and semi-official pronouncements after the Code.[10]

The authors, however, considering canon 1354, § 3, together with canon 1357, § 4, generally demand papal authority as necessary for the constitution of the regional or interdiocesan seminary. Canon 1357, § 4, seems indeed to favor such an interpretation, because it states that regional or interdiocesan seminaries are governed by special norms of the Holy See. Thus the *Directorium Seminariorum*[11] states that interdiocesan, central or regional seminaries are instituted by the authority of the Holy See alone, and that the erection of such seminaries is not in the immediate power of the Ordinaries either singly or acting as a body. Many authors adopt this same view. The erection of the interdiocesan or regional seminary is reserved to the Holy See, or, at the very least, must be ratified by the Holy See. The seminary is therefore instituted either through a formal decree of erection or through the approbation of the acts of a provincial synod ordaining its erection. This is in substance the interpretation adopted by Wernz-Vidal,[12] Coronata,[13] Brys,[14] Beste,[15] Cappello,[16] and in general by all the authors. Ver-

[10] Cf., v.g., S. C. de Sem. et Stud. Univ., *Ordinamento dei Seminari*, 26 apr. 1920—*Enchiridion Clericorum, Documenta Ecclesiae Sacrorum Alumnis Instituendis* (ed. S. Congr. de Seminariis et Studiorum Universitatibus, Romae: Typis Polyglottis Vaticanis, 1938), nos. 1080—1116 (hereafter cited *Enchiridion Clericorum*); Pius XI, litt. apost., 1 aug. 1922—*AAS*, XIV (1922), 449; Pius XI, litt. encycl. *Rerum Ecclesiae*, 28 febr. 1926—*AAS*, XVIII (1926), 65.

[11] Nos. 133, 253. The *Directorium* is not an official work, but was highly praised and recommended by the Sacred Congregation for the Propagation of the Faith. Cf. the *Directorium*, p. IX.

[12] *Ius Canonicum*, IV, ii, n. 691

[13] *Institutiones*, II, n. 935.

[14] *Iuris Canonici Compendium* (10. ed., 2 vols., Brugis: Desclée, 1947-1949), II, n. 798, 3° (hereafter cited *Compendium*).

[15] *Introductio in Codicem* (2. ed., Collegeville, Minn.: St. John's Abbey Press, 1944), p. 661 (hereafter cited *Introductio*).

[16] *Summa*, II, n. 514, 5°.

meersch—Creusen,[17] whose opinion is adopted also by Masarei,[18] state that this reservation to the Holy See does not seem to be absolute. The Council of Trent permits the provincial councils or the metropolitan with his two oldest suffragans to erect a common seminary for the Churches which cannot erect a seminary of their own. The Code of Canon Law does not expressly change or repudiate this legislation. Nor is there any evident reason why the Bishops could not, by common consent, erect a seminary of this kind. However, canon 1357, § 4, states in a universal way that interdiocesan or regional seminaries are governed by special norms of the Holy See. Since no express prohibition exists to prevent the Bishops from erecting such seminaries, the provision of canon 1357, § 4, is explained by way of fact. In fact the Bishops do not erect common seminaries—in fact the Holy See does erect them, and the seminaries are therefore governed by special norms of the Holy See.[19]

When, therefore, canon 1357, § 4, states that the interdiocesan or regional seminary is governed by special norms of the Holy See, it states primarily a fact that does exist. This is all the more evident if one considers that the Popes immediately connected with the creation, the promulgation and the first years of the new Code of Canon Law, were active in erecting regional seminaries in Italy. Pius X, Benedict XV, and Pius XI personally established no less than eleven regional seminaries for the smaller and poorer dioceses of Central and Southern Italy. *De facto* the regional seminaries were established by the Pontiffs and were governed by special norms of the Holy See.

To put the question clearly: can interdiocesan or regional seminaries in the sense of canon 1354, § 3, be instituted by the Bishops without the approval of the Holy See? We prefer to say that such seminaries, according to the present law, should be instituted by papal authority and not by the au-

[17] *Epitome,* II, n. 707.

[18] *De Missionum Institutione,* p. 274, in nota 2.

[19] Vermeersch—Creusen, *Epitome,* II, 707.

thority of the Bishops. Nevertheless it seems admissible to think that the Holy See would tolerate a situation in which the Ordinaries founded such a seminary without previously having sought papal approval. Likewise, regional or interdiocesan seminaries erected before the promulgation of the Code of Canon Law might be (and *de facto* are) allowed to function without subjection to the special norms of the Holy See.

This policy of toleration is founded on the pre-Code law and is brought out in various papal pronouncements after the Code. It has been pointed out that, before the promulgation of the Code, the law of the Council of Trent clearly permitted the Bishops to erect interdiocesan seminaries on their own authority.[20] This provision of the Council of Trent was repeatedly reiterated by the Popes and the Congregations from the time of the Council down to the promulgation of the new Code of Canon Law. As late as 1905 Pope Pius X directed Cardinal Ferrata, Prefect of the Sacred Congregation of Bishops and Regulars, to call the attention of the Bishops of Italy to the decree of the Council of Trent concerning interdiocesan seminaries, and he expressed his wish that the Bishops of dioceses by common agreement establish interdiocesan seminaries to provide for the adequate training of their clergy.[21] In 1908 the Sacred Congregation of Bishops and Regulars declared that the supreme direction of such interdiocesan seminaries pertains to the college of Bishops who use the seminaries.[22] In 1920 the Sacred Congregation of Seminaries and Universities in an instruction to the Bishops of Italy called attention also to the provision of canon 1354, § 3, and laid great stress on the obligation of the

[20] Conc. Trident., sess. XXIII, *de ref.*, c. 18—*Nova Collectio Soc. Goerr.*, IX, 628-630.

[21] Ex Chirographo *La Sacra Congregazione* ad Emum. Card. Ferrata, 16 ian. 1905—*Enchiridion Clericorum*, nos. 736-743.

[22] S. C. Episcoporum et Regularium, *Norme per l'Ordinamento Educativo e Disciplinare dei Seminari d' Italia,* Parte I, Capo 1, § 2—*Acta Sanctae Sedis* (41 vols. Romae, 1865-1908), XLI (1908), 214 (hereafter cited *ASS*).

Bishops to give their clerics a solid training elsewhere if they have no adequate seminaries of their own, but in no wise did it indicate that these seminaries can be erected by apostolic authority alone.[23]

In an Apostolic Letter of August 1, 1922, Pope Pius XI spoke of canon 1354, § 3, in such a way as to indicate that the factual interpretation of canon 1357, § 4, may be admitted. For the Pontiff urged the Bishops of poorer Churches, especially in Italy, to make use of the interdiocesan seminaries *which the Holy See has itself provided.*[24] The idea seems to be that the Holy See itself had come to the aid of the Bishops of poorer dioceses and the Holy Father expected them to take advantage of this charity.[25] Finally, in the encyclical letter *Rerum Ecclesiae,* Pius XI rejoiced in the fact that seminaries have been erected in central locations between neighboring missions which are entrusted to the same missionary order or congregation. To these seminaries the Vicars and Prefects Apostolic send their clerics, to receive them back one day as ordained priests. What therefore has been done here and there by some, the Supreme Pontiff commanded to be done by all.[26] These words, it is plain, referred to the missions. But at that time, in 1926, there existed in the Chinese missions only one regional seminary founded by apostolic authority, namely that of Ta-t'ung, whereas several central or common seminaries had already been founded through the agreement of the Vicars and Prefects Apostolic concerned. Some of these latter were to become regional seminaries governed by the special norms of the Holy See at a later date, but at the time of the encyclical letter they were not governed by these norms, and had been founded by the

[23] S. C. de Sem. et Stud. Univ., *Ordinamento dei Seminari,* ad Italiae Episcopos, 26 apr. 1920—*Enchiridion Clericorum,* nos. 1080-1116.

[24] Italics added.

[25] Pius XI, litt. apost., 1 aug. 1922—*AAS, XIV* (1922), 449.

[26] Pius XI, litt. encycl. *Rerum Ecclesiae,* 28 febr. 1926— *AAS,* XVIII (1926), 65-83.

local authorities. And, in fact, some such seminaries do exist up to the present day.

In the light of these facts it is evident that the Holy See has not insisted on a strict interpretation of the new law of the Code. At the very least, one may say that interdiocesan seminaries erected by episcopal authority before the promulgation of the Code are allowed to exist without subjection to the special norms of the Holy See. Hence, if any individual seminary of this kind functions according to its own rules, one may say that it exists validly and licitly in this way until the Holy See demands that the seminary subject itself to papal norms of administration. Likewise, although canon 1354, § 3, collated with 1357, § 4, indicates that regional seminaries may be erected only by papal authority, nevertheless since the old legislation is by no means expressly and clearly repudiated by the Code, and since the Holy See has not insisted on a strict interpretation of the present law, one may say that interdiocesan seminaries founded by episcopal authority after the Code may be tolerated and therefore be considered to exist validly and licitly, until the Holy See declares otherwise.

## Article 3. Application of the Law in Mission Lands

In article one of this chapter it was stated that, according to the uniformly accepted opinion, no juridical distinction is made between the interdiocesan and the regional seminaries spoken of in canons 1354, § 3, and 1357, § 4. The interdiocesan and regional seminaries as envisioned by these canons constitute one and the same institution.

The evolution of facts, especially in mission countries, and to be more to the point, in China, leads one to believe that in the application of the law a development has taken place. This development argues for a juridical distinction between interdiocesan and regional seminaries, so that now one may recognize three distinct types of seminaries, namely, *diocesan,* proper to one diocese; *interdiocesan,* proper to several dioceses and which have been erected by the Bishops concerned; and *regional*, proper to several dioceses, and erected and governed by the Holy See.

It has been the practice of the Congregation for the Propagation of the Faith to allow intermissional seminaries to exist in various places in China, even though such seminaries were not officially constituted by the Congregation nor governed by its special norms. Thus, although the Regional Seminary of Chi-nan (Tsinan) was erected in the Ecclesiastical Province of Shan-tung, yet the intermissional seminary of Yen-chou (Yenchow), serving the several missions of the Society of the Divine Word in Shan-tung, was allowed to exist also. In the civil province of Che-chiang (Chekiang) the Lazarists have been allowed to have the intermissional seminary of Ning-po which serves all the missions of that province. In the Province of Ssu-ch'uan (Szechwan), the Paris Foreign Mission Society has been allowed to have its intermissional seminary of Ch'eng-tu to serve the missions entrusted to the Society. These seminaries have never been recognized as regional by the Sacred Congregation for the Propagation of the Faith and have not been subjected to the regulations of the Congregation.

There were also other seminaries in China which began as seminaries of this type, but which in the course of time were constituted regional seminaries by the Sacred Congregation and placed under the special *Normae* of 1934. The Congregation had in fact opened negotiations to have the three intermissional seminaries mentioned above constituted true regional seminaries, but these negotiations were cut short by the present state of affairs in China. The fact remains however that this type of seminary is considered to form a category distinct from both diocesan seminaries and regional seminaries. The *Norme* of 1921 use only the term "regional" seminary, never "interdiocesan" or "intermissional." The *Normae* of 1934 speak only of regional, not intermissional seminaries. Likewise, the norms given by the Sacred Congregation of Seminaries and Universities for the Pontifical regional seminaries of Italy speak only of regional seminaries, and the expression "interdiocesan *or* regional" is not used.[27] Finally, the apostolic constitution *Quotidie Nos,* 11 April, 1946, distinguishes in China 12 canonically erected regional seminaries and five seminaries which are called intermissional.[28]

This usage of the Congregation seems to justify the opinion that the Holy See is willing to allow to exist, and to function according to their own rules, common seminaries which have been erected by the authority of the Bishops. These seminaries the Sacred Congregation calls "intermissional" seminaries. They are not ruled by the special *Normae* of the Sacred Congregation. On the other hand, seminaries which have been erected by the Sacred Congregation and are governed by the *Normae* are called "regional" seminaries. Thus the usage of the Sacred Congregation has introduced a juridical distinction between the regional seminary and the intermissional or interdiocesan seminary, the latter being indeed a distinct institution, founded by the agreement of the Bishops. This seminary is expected in the course of time to develop into a true regional seminary, subject to the Holy See and governed by its special norms. This doctrine was indicated as early as 1934 by the editors of the *Guida delle Missioni Cattoliche,* for they stated: "Seminari regionali sono tutti quelli dichiarati tali dalla Sacra Congregazione di Propaganda Fide e governati secondo il rescritto del 27—IV—1934—Prot.1989/34.—I seminari inter-territoriali sono seminari non dichiarati regionali dalla S.C. di Prop. Fide che di fatto contano studenti provenienti da due o più territori ecclesiastici."[29]

[27] S. C. Sem. et Stud. Univ., *Normae . . . pro Pont. Seminariis Regionalibus Italiae,* 25 mart. 1936—*Enchiridion Clericorum,* nos. 1400-1433.

[28] *AAS,* XXXVIII (1946), 302.

[29] *Guida delle Missioni Cattoliche,* 1934, p. 83.

## Article 4. The Constitution of Regional Seminaries Subject to the Sacred Congregation for the Propagation of the Faith

In this dissertation consideration is given to the regional seminary only, namely, the regional seminary *sensu iuridico,* or the one erected and governed by the Apostolic See, and there is a limitation of interest to such seminaries as are subject to the Sacred Congregation for the Propagation of the Faith. The constitution and administration of these seminaries are governed by the Regulations of 1921 if the seminary is entrusted to the secular clergy, and by the Regulations of 1934 if the seminary is committed to a religious or missionary institute. Since the Sacred Congregation favors the erection of regional seminaries under the Regulations of 1934 rather than under those of 1921, and since fourteen of the fifteen regional seminaries in China are entrusted to a missionary or religious institute, it seems fully indicated to follow the order of the Regulations of 1934 in the present commentary. The commentary shall be divided into four chapters and shall follow the division of the Regulations, namely: Supreme Direction; Rights and Duties of the Superior General of the Institute; Rights and Duties of the Ordinaries of the Region; and the Rights and Duties of the Rector. The last article of each chapter will be devoted to the *Norme* of 1921 and will point out the differences between the two sets of norms.

Before going on to the commentary on these norms, one should here enumerate the steps to be taken for the erection of a regional seminary. The commentary on these points will be found in the proper places in the chapters which follow. The constitution of a regional seminary calls for the following:

1. Preparatory Acts—The Ordinaries first agree to the erection of such a seminary, choose a site for the seminary, and find a religious institute willing to accept the administration. The Ordinaries then communicate their proposal to the Sacred Congregation for the Propagation of the Faith,

either through the Apostolic Nuncio in China[30] or, if all or the majority of the Ordinaries concerned are of the same religious or missionary order, perhaps through the agency of the Superior General of their institute. The Sacred Congregation then offers the administration of the seminary to a religious institute, and upon receiving a favorable reply, and provided that all other matters are favorably resolved, proceeds to the decree of erection.

2. The Decree of Erection—The Sacred Congregation for the Propagation of the Faith erects the regional seminary through a formal decree, committing the studies, discipline, and ordinary administration to the care of the religious or missionary institute which has agreed to accept the administration upon the invitation of the same Congregation.[31]

3. The Economic Agreement—The ordinaries of the region and the Superior General of the institute then enter into an agreement as to the economic administration of the seminary. The agreement determines how the expenses of the seminary are to be met, what funds are to be placed at the disposal of the seminary, etc., and gives exact rules on the administration of the funds.[32]

4. Election of the Rector, Officials, and Professors—A candidate for the office of rector is first presented by the Superior General of the religious institute, and is then appointed to the office by means of a letter or decree of the Sacred Congregation for the Propagation of the Faith.[33]

The appointment of the other officials and of the professors is made by the Superior General of the religious institute, and the list of appointments is sent to the Sacred Congregation. These officials and professors are therefore appointed, not by the Congregation, but by the religious institute.[34]

[30] *Directorium,* n. 253.
[31] *Normae* (1934), n. 1—*Sylloge,* n. 183.
[32] *Normae* (1934), n. 9—*Sylloge,* n. 183.
[33] *Normae* (1934), n. 4, a)—*Sylloge,* n. 183.
[34] *Normae* (1934), nos. 4, b) and 7—*Sylloge,* n. 183.

5. Approval of the *Regulae* etc.—The institute to which the government of the seminary is entrusted draws up the rules of discipline, the program of studies, the arrangement of the subjects, the scholastic *horarium,* and the list of textbooks. These are then submitted to the Sacred Congregation for the Propagation of the Faith for examination, and are definitely approved, after emendation, in a letter of the same Congregation.[85] Normally all this should be done either before the seminary is officially opened or during the first year of existence. Therefore these matters are to be expedited as soon as there is convenient opportunity for the persons concerned.

[85] *Normae* (1934), n. 3—*Sylloge,* n. 183.

## CHAPTER V

## THE SUPREME DIRECTION OF REGIONAL SEMINARIES

Text

### I. De Alta Directione

1. Seminarium Regionale pertinet ad Sanctam Sedem, quae eius gubernium alicui Instituto Religioso vel Missionali committit sub alta tamen directione Sacrae Congregationis de Propaganda Fide. Disciplina Seminarii eius scholae et ordinaria administratio relinquuntur curae Instituti.

2. Seminarium comprehendit cursum Philosophicum duorum saltem annorum et cursum Theologicum quattuor annorum.

3. Institutum cui committitur directio Seminarii Regionalis Sacrae Congregationi de Propaganda Fide submittet adprobandas:

a) Regulas disciplinares Seminarii.

b) Rationem studiorum, distributionem disciplinarum, horarium scholasticum et notam librorum textus.

4. a) Electio Rectoris Seminarii ad Sacram Congregationem de Propaganda spectat post praesentationem candidati ex parte Superioris Generalis Instituti.

b) Electio coeterorum moderatorum necnon professorum spectat ad Superiorem Generalem Instituti, qui postea eorum nomina Sacrae Congregationi de Propaganda communicabit.

c) Remotio vel mutatio Rectoris Seminarii fieri non potest absque praevio consensu Sacrae Congregationis de Propaganda; mutatio professorum aliorumque moderatorum communicabitur eidem Sacrae Congregationi.

5. Ad Seminarium Regionale ordinarie pergent omnes alumni Philosophiae et Theologiae Regionis. Ordinariis non licebit ex Seminario Regionali suos alumnos revocare eosque alio educandos mittere, sine expressa licentia Sacrae Congregationis de Propaganda Fide.

6. Alumni Seminarii qui in vocatione ecclesiastica perseverant, nequibunt vel in cursu studiorum vel ante triennium completum a suo sacerdotio in aliquod religiosum Institutum introire, absque peculiari licentia proprii Ordinarii et Sanctae Sedis, firmis manentibus quae statuuntur cann. 981, § 1, et 542 C.I.C.[1]

Translation

I. Supreme Direction

1. The regional seminary belongs to the Holy See, which entrusts the government of it to a religious or missionary institute under the supreme direction of the Sacred Congregation for the Propagation of the Faith. To the institute are committed the discipline, studies, and ordinary administration.

2. The seminary has a course of at least two years in philosophy, and of four years in theology.

3. The institute to which the direction of the regional seminary is entrusted shall submit to the Sacred Congregation for the Propagation of the Faith for approval:

a) The disciplinary regulations of the seminary;

b) the program of studies, the arrangement of the subjects, the scholastic *horarium,* and a list of textbooks.

4. a) The election of the rector of the seminary pertains to the Sacred Congregation for the Propagation of the Faith upon the presentation of a candidate by the Superior General of the institute;

b) the election of the other officials and professors pertains to the Superior General of the institute, who shall however communicate their names [that is, his appointments] to the Sacred Congregation for the Propagation of the Faith;

c) it is the right of the same Sacred Congregation to change or remove the rector of the seminary; any change made in professors or in other superiors must be communicated to the same Sacred Congregation.

[1] *Normae* (1934)—*Sylloge,* n. 183. Numbers 1, 5 and 6 of the *Normae* are considered in this chapter; numbers 2-4 (studies, discipline, professors and officials) are treated in chapter six of this dissertation.

5. Ordinarily all students of philosophy and theology in the region must be sent to the regional seminary; the Ordinaries may not withdraw their students from this regional seminary in order to educate them elsewhere without the express permission of the Sacred Congregation for the Propagation of the Faith.

6. The students of the seminary who persevere in their ecclesiastical vocation may not enter a religious institute—neither during the course of studies, nor before the lapse of three full years from their ordination to the priesthood—without the special consent of their own Ordinary and of the Holy See, without prejudice also to the provisions of canons 981, § 1, and 542 of the Code of Canon Law.

## Article 1. The Rights of the Sacred Congregation for the Propagation of the Faith

The regional seminary erected according to the provisions of the *Normae* of 1934 belongs to the Holy See and is subject to the Sacred Congregation for the Propagation of the Faith. By the authority of the Holy See, the Sacred Congregation entrusts the government of the seminary to a religious or missionary institute, but reserves to itself the right of supervision over the seminary's disciplinary, scholastic and economic administration. The Sacred Congregation exercises this right of supervision by approving the rules of discipline and the program of studies, by appointing the rector of the seminary, by approving the appointments of professors and moderators, by demanding an accurate annual report of the entire spiritual and temporal administration of the seminary. The Sacred Congregation also exercises the right of supreme supervision by demanding that all the students of the region served by the regional seminary be sent to this seminary and not elsewhere except by special permission; finally, by forbidding the students to enter a religious institute until three full years have elapsed from their ordination to the priesthood.[2]

[2] *Normae* (1934), nos. 1-6, 12—*Sylloge*, n. 183.

It is stated in n. 1 of the *Normae* that the Holy See entrusts the government of the seminary to a religious or missionary institute. Just how this is done has been demonstrated in the history of the constitution of 15 regional seminaries in China. When the Ordinaries of a region come to an agreement with the Sacred Congregation for the Propagation of the Faith concerning the erection of a regional seminary, the Sacred Congregation offers the administration of the seminary to that religious institute which the Ordinaries have suggested. If the institute accepts this invitation, the official decree of erection commits the government of the seminary to this institute, entrusting to it the studies, the discipline, the administration of temporalities. Thereafter the institute governs the seminary according to the provisions of the *Normae* of 1934.[3]

According to n. 1 of the *Normae* the regional seminary belongs to the Holy See. The evident meaning of this provision

[3] The following may serve as an example of a typical decree of erection:

DECRETUM

Cum Reverendissimi Ordinarii Ecclesiasticae Provinciae Nganhoeivensis (Anhwei), in Sinis, supplices ad hanc Sacram Congregationem porrexerint preces ut maius seminarium in dioecesi Uhuvensi (Wuhu) existens in SEMINARIUM REGIONALE ad normam sacrorum canonum constituatur; haec eadem Sacra Congregatio de Propaganda Fide, praehabita favorabili ad rem sententia Exc. mi Apostolici in Sinis Delegati, necnon Rev. mi P. Praepositi Generalis Societatis Iesu, cui idem seminarium est committendum, seminarium maius in urbe vulgo *Shuencheng* existens in SEMINARIUM REGIONALE pro Missionibus Provinciae Ecclesiasticae Nganhoeivensis erigit et constituit cum omnibus iuribus et privilegiis huiusmodi piis institutis a lege recognitis, idemque Patribus Societatis Iesu committit, iuxta regulas ab hac Sacra Congregatione emanatas regendum, atque in huiusce rei memoriam statuit ut praesens conficeretur Decretum.

Datum Romae, ex Aedibus Sacrae Congregationis de Propaganda Fide, die XIII mensis Iunii, anno Domini 1947.

Petrus Card. Fumasoni-Biondi, Praefectus
✠ Celsus Constantini, a Secretis.

*Archivum S. C. P. F.*, Wu-hu, a. 1947.

of the regulations is that in ecclesiastical law the ownership of the seminary is vested in the Apostolic See. The buildings used for the regional seminary may have been erected precisely for the purpose of housing the regional seminary, and perhaps by funds donated by the Pontifical Work of St. Peter for the Native Clergy, or, as is the case with several regional seminaries in China, the buildings may have been erected by the local Ordinary for some other purpose, and turned over to the regional seminary at a later date. But no matter what the origin of the buildings has been (whether erected by the local Ordinary or by several Ordinaries or by a religious institute), when the buildings become the seat of the regional seminary, they become at the same time the property of the Holy See. This transfer of property may be formal and explicit, or virtual and implicit. It would be formal if the diocese, vicariate, or religious institute which owned the buildings either entered into a contract of sale with the Holy See, or explicitly donated the property to the Holy See. The transfer of property would be virtual if the diocese or institute which owned the buildings accepted the fact that the property was to become the seat of a regional seminary erected according to the *Normae* of 1934. This would be equivalent to a donation of the property to the Holy See, for the norms according to which the regional seminary is to be erected state that the seminary belongs to the Holy See. The acceptance of this fact contains a virtual and implicit transfer of the property rights to the Holy See by donation. This, then, seems to be the true meaning of n. 1 of the *Normae,* and appears quite conformable to the mind of the Apostolic See, which would not constitute a regional seminary in buildings which remained in the ownership of an individual diocese or institute. For the regional seminary, which is common to several missions, ought not to be dependent upon a particular Ordinary or on a religious institute, but on the Holy See alone.

This interpretation of n. 1 of the *Normae* is confirmed by the particular provisions of several economic agreements between the Ordinaries for the administration of regional seminaries. In the agreement of the Ordinaries for the Regional Seminary of Hsiang-kang (Hongkong), it is stated that the ownership of the seminary pertains to the Sacred Congregation for the Propagation of the Faith, but that the use of it belongs to the Vicars Apostolic of the region.[4] In the agreement between the Ordinaries of the Ecclesiastical Province of Fu-chien (Fukien) and the Order of Preachers for the Regional Seminary of Fu-chien, it is stated that the ownership of the seminary pertains to the Holy See, the use, however, to the Ordinaries of the region of Fu-chien.[5] Even in the general statutes drawn up by the Fathers of Scheut as early as 1921, it is stated that the seminary once erected will constitute, with all its movable and immovable goods, the property of the Sacred Congregation for the Propagation of the Faith.[6]

### *Ownership in Civil Law*

According to civil law, the regional seminary is held as property of the diocese in which the seminary is located. In practice, generally all Church property, including regional seminaries, is registered with the Land Office as property of the Catholic Church of that district, either as evincing ownership or as involving a perpetual lease. In the eyes of the civil law, therefore, the regional seminary is considered the property of the Catholic mission (diocese, vicariate, prefecture) in which the seminary is located. Consequently in the economic agreement between the Ordinaries of the region and the religious institutes to which the regional seminaries are entrusted, it is usually stated that the legal

[4] "Conventio Ordinariorum pro Seminario Regionali de Hongkong," n. 5—*Archivum S. C. P. F.*, Hsiang-kang (Hongkong), n. 1299/27 prot.

[5] "Conventio . . . inter Ordinarios Regionis Eccl. de Fukien et Ordinem Praedicatorum," n. 1—*Archivum S. C. P. F.*, Fu-chou, n. 3102/37 prot.

[6] "Projet d'Organisation et d'Administration du Seminaire Central de Tatung," n. 4—*Archivum S. C. P. F.*, n. 1025/21 prot., rub. 130.

representative of the seminary before the civil government is the local Ordinary.[7]

## Article 2. Attendance at the Regional Seminary

Number 5 of the *Normae*[8] contains two separate provisions regarding attendance at the regional seminary. In the first place it is stated that all the students of philosophy and theology from the region shall ordinarily be sent to the regional seminary. This is evident, for the regional seminary has been erected to serve the needs of the region. It is said that *ordinarily* all shall go to the regional seminary. Evidently exceptions may be made, and an individual Bishop is free to send one or the other student elsewhere without any special permission. This conclusion is admitted by all the authors, and there is no reason to question it.

Secondly, number 5 states that the Ordinaries are not allowed to withdraw their students from the regional seminary to send them elsewhere without the express permission of the Sacred Congregation. This provision of the *Normae* refers, it seems, not to an individual case wherein a student is taken out of the regional seminary to be educated elsewhere, but rather to a matter of policy, whereby a Bishop abandons the regional seminary and sends all his students to some other seminary. This is forbidden by number 5 of

[7] Cf., v. g., "Conventio . . . inter Ordinarios Regionis Eccl. de Fukien et Ordinem Praedicatorum," n. 1—*Archivum S. C. P. F.*, Fu-chou, n. 3102/37 prot. Information as to the property rights of the Catholic Church in China may be gathered from the following sources: Grentrup, *Ius Missionarium* (Steyl-Holland: Typographia domus Missionum a S. Michaele Arch., 1925), p. 146 (hereafter cited *Ius*); "Constitutiones Provisoriae Gubernii Nankingensis circa Bona Missionum (Die 20 Iulii 1928)"—*Coll. Comm. Syn.*, I (1928), 365-367; "Mission Property Laws," *op. cit.*, II (1929), 140; "De Bonis Missionum," *op. cit.*, IV (1931), 601-608.

[8] "Ad Seminarium Regionale ordinarie pergent omnes alumni Philosophiae et Theologiae Regionis. Ordinariis non licebit ex Seminario Regionali suos alumnos revocare eosque alio educandos mittere, sine expressa licentia Sacrae Congregationis de Propaganda Fide."—*Sylloge*, n. 183.

the *Normae*. To do this a Bishop of the region who is served by the regional seminary needs the express permission of the Sacred Congregation.

The term "region" in this provision of the regulations must be taken in a relative sense. It should not be taken to mean an ecclesiastical or civil province. One might be misled by the fact that prior to 1946 China was divided into ecclesiastical *regions*.[9] In the *Normae*, however, the term "region" signifies the territory that is constituted by the dioceses for which the particular regional seminary has been erected; it is the composite of the dioceses served by the regional seminary according to its decree of erection. For example, the region of the Regional Seminary of Ching-hsien (Kinghsien) embraces only a part of the Ecclesiastical Province of Ho-pei (Hopeh), namely, the Dioceses of Ching-hsien, Hsien-hsien (Sienhsien), Ta-ming, and Yung-nien. The region of the Regional Seminary of Fu-chien (Fukien) embraces the entire Ecclesiastical Province of Fu-chien (Fukien) The region of the Regional Seminary of Han-k'ou (Hankow) embraces the two Ecclesiastical Provinces of Hu-pei (Hupeh) and Hu-nan.[10]

A Bishop must obtain the permission of the Sacred Congregation to send his students elsewhere only if a regional seminary has been erected for the service also of his diocese. Otherwise no such permission is necessary, even though a regional seminary actually exists in the province. Thus the Ordinaries of the missions entrusted to the Society of the Divine Word in Shan-tung province are not obliged to send their students to the Regional Seminary of Chi-nan (Tsinan), for this seminary was erected for the Franciscan missions of the Shan-tung province, the Society of the Divine Word missions using their own intermissional seminary of Yen-chou (Yenchow).

The *Normae* state however that with the proper permission Ordinaries may send their students to a seminary other

[9] *PCS—Vota et Postulata*, n. 2.

[10] Consult chapter III, article 3, nos. 5, 13, 14, of this dissertation.

than the regional seminary which serves their dioceses.[11] As examples one may consider the following. The Regional Seminary of T'ai-yüan was erected in 1935 upon the request of the Ordinaries of four Franciscan missions of Shan-hsi province. The Sacred Congregation however demanded that this seminary serve as the regional seminary for the Ecclesiastical Region (now Province) of Shan-hsi, so that the missions of Fen-yang and Hung-tung, entrusted to the native secular clergy, would also have the right to send their students to this seminary. At the same time the Congregation declared these two missions not to be under obligation to send their students to the Regional Seminary of T'ai-yüan, but to have the right to do so if it so pleases them.[12] And so, although the Regional Seminary of T'ai-yüan was erected for the Ecclesiastical Province of Shan-hsi, yet two missions of that province are given an option. They may send their students to this seminary if they wish, or elsewhere if they consider that more opportune. In fact, the two missions continued to send their students to the Regional Seminary of Süan-hua, since it was entrusted to the native secular clergy.[13]

Another example is had in the case of the Diocese of Hsü-chou (Süchow). In 1947 the Regional Seminary of Shang-hai was erected for the Ecclesiastical Province of Chiang-su (Kiangsu).[14] Before that date the Diocese of Hsü-chou had sent its students to the Regional Seminary of Ching-hsien (Kinghsien) in Ho-pei province, because the climate and food there were considered better for the students' health. When the Regional Seminary of Shang-hai was erected for all the missions of Chiang-su province, the Apostolic Nuncio in China, Archbishop Antonio Riberi, wished the students of the Diocese of Hsü-chou to attend this seminary, and he

[11] *Normae* (1934), n. 5—*Sylloge*, n. 183.

[12] S. C. P. F., litt., 11 ian. 1935—*Archivum S. C. P. F.*, T'ai-yüan, n. 4804/34 prot.

[13] *Annuaire*, 1935-1947.

[14] S. C. P. F., decr., 7 nov. 1947—*Archivum S. C. P. F.*, Shang-hai, a. 1947.

hoped to provide them with the living conditions they needed. However, the Sacred Congregation in a letter of November 12, 1947, expressed doubt as to the remedy proposed, and therefore preferred to see the students of Hsü-chou continue to frequent the Regional Seminary of Ching-hsien or some other seminary which beyond question proved healthful for the students.[15] Thus the Diocese of Hsü-chou (Süchow) has permission to send its students to another seminary, and need not send them to the seminary of its own region.

These few examples will suffice to show that the Sacred Congregation is willing to grant permission to the Ordinaries to send their students to other seminaries. Good reasons must be advanced for the granting of the permission, such as the health of the students, education in a definite tradition, close ties of friendship between a mother mission and its filial missions, etc. The law on attendance at regional seminaries may be summarized as follows:

1. The term "region" one must take as signifying that territory or that composite of dioceses for which the seminary is officially erected. If a diocese is one of those for which the regional seminary has been erected, permission of the Sacred Congregation is required before the students of the diocese may as a matter of policy be sent elsewhere.

2. No permission is required for the sending of one or the other student to a seminary other than the proper regional seminary.

3. If a regional seminary is erected for only some, but not all, of the dioceses of an ecclesiastical province, these other dioceses are not bound to send their students to the regional seminary.

4. If a diocese is not included within the region served by a regional seminary, the Bishop may send his students to a seminary of his choice according to the provisions of canon 1354, § 3, of the Code of Canon Law.

[15] S. C. P. F., litt., 12 nov. 1947—*Archivum S. C. P. F.*, Wu-hu, n. 3157/47 prot.

### Article 3. Prohibition against Entrance into a Religious Institute

The students of the seminary who persevere in their ecclesiastical vocation may not enter a religious institute—neither during the course of studies, nor before the lapse of three full years from their ordination to the priesthood—without the special consent of their own Ordinary and of the Holy See, without prejudice also to the provisions of canons 981, § 1, and 542 of the Code of Canon Law.[16]

The encyclical letters of the Popes, the instructions of the Congregations, and the decrees of the Councils recommend that the religious life and religious vocations be fostered in mission lands, and that new religious institutes be founded which are more consonant with the genius of particular peoples and nations.[17] Nevertheless, it remains the purpose of the regional seminary to form a native secular clergy and therefore the *Normae* include this provision which forbids entrance of the students into a religious institute. The prohibition is however a temporary one, which ceases upon the completion of the third year after ordination to the priesthood. Likewise, the prohibition is not absolute, for with the proper permission the student or young priest is allowed to enter religion before the expiration of the prohibitory period. The purpose of this prohibition is to provide for the common good, namely, the propagation of the faith and the salvation of souls. If a cleric wishes to enter a religious order the Holy See and the local Ordinary have the right to decide whether the salvation of souls will suffer by the cleric's departure from the ranks of the secular clergy. In short, the public good must be preferred to the private good of the cleric, and for this reason the *Normae* have included the present prohibition.[18]

This provision of the *Normae* has a long and venerated

[16] *Normae* (1934), n. 6—*Sylloge*, n. 183.

[17] Pius XI, litt. encycl. *Rerum Ecclesiae*, 28 febr. 1926— *AAS*, XVIII (1926), 65-83; *PCS*, nos. 174-175, 647.

[18] Cf. S. C. P. F., instr., 27 apr. 1871, n. 10—*Fontes*, n. 4878.

history, for it is no doubt inspired by the "Alexandrian oath" imposed on the students of Pontifical Colleges subject to the Sacred Congregation for the Propagation of the Faith. According to this oath, the students promise to return to their homeland to work in the sacred ministry after ordination, and not to enter a religious order, society or congregation without the special permission of the Holy See, either while they are in the college or after they have left it, their studies being completed or not. This oath was first prescribed by Urban VIII,[19] augmented later by Alexander VII,[20] the latest formula of the oath being drawn up by the Sacred Congregation for the Propagation of the Faith in 1910.[21] This oath constituted a diriment impediment to entrance into religion, for any reception or profession made contrary to its provisions was null and void.[22]

The "Alexandrian oath" has not been imposed on the students of regional seminaries; instead, the *Normae,* in number 6, contain a simple prohibition by which it is unlawful for the students to enter religion. This provision does not invalidate entrance into religion if perhaps it is done without the proper permission, but does render the same illicit, as is evident.

The *Normae* further state that this provision of number 6 does not in any way change or modify the law of the Code as contained in canons 981, § 1, and 542.[23] The provisions of canons 981, § 1, and 542, therefore, retain their full force in regard to the students of regional seminaries subject to the Sacred Congregation for the Propagation of the Faith. According to canon 981, § 1, if not even one of the titles for promotion to sacred orders enumerated in canon 979, § 1 (benefice, patrimony, subsidy), is at hand, it may be supplied by the title of "service of the diocese," and in places

[19] S. C. P. F., C. G., 24 nov. 1625—*Fontes,* n. 4430.
[20] Const., 20 iul. 1660—*Coll. S. C. P. F.,* n. 142.
[21] Decr., 19 febr. 1910—*Sylloge,* n. 226 bis.
[22] S. C. P. F., C. G., 24 nov. 1625—*Fontes,* n. 4430.
[23] *Normae* (1934), n. 6—*Sylloge,* n. 183.

subject to the Sacred Congregation for the Propagation of the Faith, by the title "of the mission." However, a candidate ordained under either of these titles must take the oath to devote his entire life to the service of the diocese or mission under the authority of the Ordinary of the place.[24]

When a cleric in China is promoted to the subdiaconate under the title "of the mission," he must take the oath to devote his life to the service of the mission according to the formula prescribed by the Sacred Congregation for the Propagation of the Faith as contained in the instruction of the 27th of April, 1871.[25] According to this formula of the oath, the cleric swears to work in the mission for life under the jurisdiction of the local Ordinary, and not to enter a religious order, society or congregation without the special permission of the Holy See, nor to make profession in any of them.[26]

Canon 542 of the Code of Canon Law states that, if by a disposition of the Holy See, clerics are bound by oath to devote themselves to the service of their diocese or of the missions, they cannot be validly admitted to the novitiate for that period of time for which their oath binds them.[27] Accordingly there arises the question whether or not the clerics who take the oath prescribed by canon 981, § 1, are debarred from the religious life by canon 542, 1°. The formula of the oath demanded by canon 981, § 1, is not determined by the common law. It seems sufficient that the oath make mention of the fact that the cleric to be ordained will serve the diocese or mission perpetually under the authority of the local Ordinary. However, since this oath is demanded by the common law, it will not constitute the diriment impediment of canon 542, 1°. For in that canon there is question of an oath demanded by special disposition of the Holy See, and not of the oath prescribed by the common law of the

[24] Can. 981, § 1.

[25] *PCS*, n. 369.

[26] Ex instr. S. C. P. F., die 27 apr. 1871—*Fontes*, n. 4878.

[27] Can. 542, 1°.

Church. In fact, the oath of canon 981, § 1, does not even constitute an impedient impediment, for its obligation would cease by the very fact that the cleric wishes to embrace a more perfect life.[28]

Canon 542, 1°, refers primarily to the oath which by special disposition of the Holy See must be made by the students of some seminaries and colleges which educate priests for mission lands. For the members of not a few Pontifical Colleges, upon entrance to the institution, are required to take the oath of perpetual service of the diocese or mission to which they will be sent, and of not entering a religious institute. This oath therefore comprehends more than that which is demanded by canon 981, § 1, and implies in fact a special law for these Pontifical Colleges.

With regard to others who are not members of the colleges mentioned above, but who are ordained *titulo missionis*, the fact remains that the formula used for the oath to be taken before one is ordained under this title, and still in use up to this time, contains not only that clause which the common law imposes in canon 981, § 1, i.e., to devote oneself to the perpetual service of the mission, but also the clause imposed by special disposition of the Holy See, i.e., the clause forbidding entrance into a religious institute. The very text of the instruction of the Sacred Congregation for the Propagation of the Faith by which this formula of the oath was imposed on those to be ordained under the title "of the mission" indicates that the oath is to be interpreted in the same manner as the oath taken by those who study in the Pontifical Colleges,[29] and therefore, as constituting a diriment impedi-

[28] Beste, *Introductio*, pp. 528, 361; Vermeersch—Creusen, *Epitome*, I, n. 680; Brys, *Compendium*, I, n. 635; Coronata, *Institutiones Iuris Canonici ad Usum Utriusque Cleri et Scholarum, de Sacramentis, Tractatus Canonicus* (3 vols. Romae: Marietti, 1943-1946), II, n. 91 (hereafter cited *De Sacramentis*); Schaefer, *De Religiosis* (4. ed., Romae: Typis Polyglottis Vaticanis, 1947), n. 799; Wernz—Vidal, *Ius Canonicum*, III, n. 253.

[29] "Non secus ac alumni Collegiorum pontificiorum, ii omnes qui titulo Missionis inter sacros ministros cooptari cupiunt, tenentur

ment to the valid entrance into religion.[30] If therefore the Holy See either demands the oath in this form or permits that it be demanded in this form, the final clause of canon 542, 1°, seems to be verified, namely, that by special disposition of the Holy See the cleric is bound by oath to devote himself to the service of the missions, and is therefore forbidden to enter religion under penalty of nullity of the act.[31]

The Holy See permits the oath to be taken in China according to the formula which forbids entrance into religion, for in the decrees of the First Plenary Council of China, it

prius iuramentum emittere, quo spondeant Missioni cui destinati sunt vel destinabuntur, se fore perpetuam operam daturos; quod quidem ab iis qui hoc titulo frui volunt, S. Sedes, ut Missionum, quarum sumptibus illi aluntur, servitio consuleret, exigere constanter consuevit. Huic Instructioni subnectitur Forma istius iuramenti iampridem approbata usuque recepta, eamque ab omnibus usurpandam esse, ut uniformitas hac super re servetur, omnino praecipit S. Congregatio.... Eis, qui hoc titulo sunt ordinati, vi praestiti iuramenti interdicitur in Religionem ingredi absque venia S. Sedis; eius namque iudicio reservatum est, praevia Ordinarii, cui intererit, relatione, iudicare utrum Missionum, quarum servitio ii sunt addicti, necessitas id patiatur. Scilicet publicum bonum privato antecellat opportet, ea nimirum ratione, qua aliquibus Ordinibus concessum est, ne eorum religiosis ad arctiorem sine suorum Superiorum licentia transire fas sit."—S. C. P. F., instr., 27 apr. 1871, nos. 8 and 10—*Fontes*, n. 4878. Concerning this whole question one must bear in mind that the origin of the title "of the mission" was very closely connected with the oath demanded of the students in Pontifical Colleges.

[30] "Praeterea de mandato similiter speciali eiusdem S. D. N. [Urbani VIII] statuit, et decernit [Sacra Congregatio de Propaganda Fide] neminem deinceps praedictorum alumnorum contra infrascriptam iuramenti formulam in aliqua Religione, Societate et Congregatione Regulari a superioribus recipi, nec ad professionem admitti posse vel debere; alioquin receptio, et professio nullae sint, ac nullius roboris, et firmitatis...."—S. C. P. F., C. G., 24 nov. 1625—*Fontes*, n. 4430.

[31] Coronata, *De Sacramentis*, II, n. 92; Schaefer, *De Religiosis*, n. 800. See also: Paventi, *De Iuramento ac de Titulo Missionis* (Romae: Officium Libri Catholici, 1946), pp. 79-82; Larraona, "Commentarium Codicis—Can. 542, 1° (cont.) et 2°," *Commentarium pro Religiosis et Missionariis*, XVII (1936), 236-246.

is stated that any cleric to be ordained *titulo missionis* must, before he receives the subdiaconate, take the oath according to the customary formula prescribed by the Sacred Congregation for the Propagation of the Faith in the instruction of the 27th of April, 1871.[32] Hence those students of the regional seminaries in China who are to be ordained under the title "of the mission" must before the subdiaconate take the oath prescribed by canon 981, § 1, according to the formula of the instruction of 1871, and are therefore excluded from entering religion according to the provision of canon 542, 1°. This conclusion is true only of the clerics ordained to *major* orders *titulo missionis;* not of those in minor orders, nor of those who are ordained under the title of patrimony, subsidy or benefice.

Finally, canon 542 in its second section states that it is unlawful for clerics in sacred orders to enter the novitiate without consulting the local Ordinary, or against his will if his objection be based on the serious harm to souls that the withdrawal of the clerics would cause, when this harm cannot be averted by other means.[33] This provision concerning the licit entrance into the novitiate, being sufficiently clear from the uniform explanation furnished by the authors, needs no special consideration here.[34]

### Article 4. Differences in the *Norme* of 1921

The rules for the supreme direction of regional seminaries erected according to the provisions of the *Norme* of 1921 do not differ greatly from the rules for the government of seminaries entrusted to a religious or missionary institute. The two sets of rules, or norms, have the following points in common: the regional seminary is placed under the supreme supervision of the Sacred Congregation for the Propagation of the Faith; the Sacred Congregation approves the

[32] *PCS*, n. 369.

[33] Can. 542, 2°.

[34] See, v. g., Coronata, *Institutiones*, I, n. 571; Brys, *Compendium*, I, n. 635; Schaefer, *De Religiosis*, nos. 802-803.

rules of discipline, the program of studies, the textbooks; the Congregation appoints the rector, and must be informed of the appointments of other officials and professors; all the students of the region served by the seminary must make their philosophical and theological studies there, and not be sent elsewhere except by special permission of the Sacred Congregation.[35] As the *Normae* of 1934 call for an agreement between the Ordinaries and the religious institute regarding the economic administration, so the *Norme* of 1921 demand that the Ordinaries of the region submit for approval to the Sacred Congregation a document stating an estimate of the seminary's income, an appraisal of the amount of money to be contributed by the individual missions, and an estimate of the funds necessary to operate the seminary.[36]

The *Norme* however do not contain any provision forbidding the students to enter a religious institute. But if a regional seminary were to be erected and entrusted to the secular clergy, a special provision to that effect could be placed in the special rules for the government of the seminary. The Ordinaries of Japan have petitioned and received from the Sacred Congregation for the Propagation of the Faith the right to demand an oath of the students of the Regional Seminary of Tokyo not to enter the religious life without the permission of the Holy See.[37] This seminary is entrusted to the secular clergy.

For the rest, let it suffice to say that the *Norme* of 1921 do not have wide application today. These norms were made, as their title indicates, for China,[38] not for other lands subject to the Sacred Congregation for the Propagation of the Faith. Since the *Norme* were first drawn up in 1921, only one regional seminary in China has been entrusted to the

[35] *Norme* (1921), nos. 1-4—Part III (Documents), Document 3.

[36] *Norme* (1921), n. 2 d—Part III (Documents), Document 3.

[37] S. C. P. F., epistola, 1 apr. 1942—*Archivum S. C. P. F.*, n. 489/42 prot., rub. 35/3.

[38] "Norme per i Seminari Regionali in Cina."

secular clergy, all the others being entrusted to a religious or missionary institute, and consequently governed by the *Normae* of 1934. If any regional seminary were erected today and the administration of the same committed to the care of the secular clergy, the *Norme* of 1921 would indeed serve as the basis for the rules of administration for the seminary, but the regulations would in all probability be brought up to date and include several provisions not contained in the redaction of 1921.

## CHAPTER VI

## RIGHTS AND DUTIES OF THE SUPERIOR GENERAL OF THE INSTITUTE

Text

II. De Iuribus et Officiis Superioris Generalis Instituti

7. Nominatio et munerum attributio omnium superiorum et magistrorum Seminarii (salvo praescripto art. 4, a), remittitur curae Superioris Generalis Instituti.

8. Director Spiritus alumnorum nunquam seligetur ex moderatoribus Seminarii, idemque intra septa Instituti residentiam continuam habebit.

9. Superior Generalis cum Ordinariis Regionis circa administrativam gestionem Seminarii conveniet.[1]

Translation

II. Rights and Duties of the Superior General of the Institute

7. The selection of the directing and teaching staff and the distribution of offices among the officials and teachers of the seminary are committed to the care of the Superior General of the institute (without prejudice however to the provision of art. 4, a).

8. The spiritual director assigned to the students shall never be chosen from the ranks of the superiors of the seminary; and he shall have permanent residence within the walls of the seminary.

9. The Superior General shall come to an agreement with the Ordinaries of the region regarding the temporal [economic] administration of the seminary.

### Article 1. Appointment of Officials and Professors

The *Normae* of 1934 give to the Superior General of the religious or missionary institute the right to present a can-

[1] *Normae* (1934)—*Sylloge,* n. 183.

didate for the office of rector and to appoint the other officials and the professors. The appointments made by the Superior General do not require the approbation of the Sacred Congregation for the Propagation of the Faith, but the Congregation must be informed of the appointments made. The rector is appointed by the Congregation, and once appointed cannot be removed or changed without the previous consent of the Congregation. The other officials and professors may be removed by the Superior General without permission, but the Congregation must be informed of the changes made.[2]

The Superior General need not consult the Ordinaries of the region when making his appointments, but prudence and practical considerations suggest that he do so. For the officials and professors of the regional seminary will usually be chosen from the ranks of the religious who are already in the missions served by the seminary. The Mission Superior therefore must know if priests of his mission are to be called away from their present duties. Although it is usually the prerogative of the Superior General of the institute both to send religious to the missions and to recall them or to transfer them from one mission to another,[3] yet these things he should not undertake to do without first consulting the local Ordinaries concerned.[4]

The number and distinction of officials and professors to be appointed are determined by the Code of Canon Law and the nature of the institution. In every seminary there should be a rector for discipline, teachers for instruction, a procurator, distinct from the rector, for the financial administration, at least two ordinary confessors, and a spiritual director.[5] To these may be added the vice-rector for the more immediate control of the discipline, the prefect of studies for the management of the scholastic program, and extra-

[2] *Normae* (1934), nos. 7, 4—*Sylloge*, n. 183.

[3] Cf., v. g., *Statuta pro Missionibus Ordinis Fratrum Minorum* (Ad Claras Aquas: ex Typographia Collegii S. Bonaventurae, 1950), n. 4d (hereafter cited *Statuta O.F.M.*).

[4] *Statuta O.F.M.*, n. 8h.

[5] Can. 1358.

ordinary confessors to whom the students may freely go.

In the missions these offices are to be filled as well as they can be, for although one of the purposes of regional seminaries is to have a more complete staff than is possible in individual diocesan seminaries, yet it may well be that even here it is sometimes impossible to have all that the law calls for.[6] For this reason the Superior General may request that one or the other native secular priest be made available for a position in the regional seminary, for nothing would prohibit the Superior General from appointing to a position a priest not of his institute, especially a native priest. This will of course require the consent of the Ordinary of the priest to be appointed. The Superior General could also appoint to the seminary those of his subjects who have not been in the mission field. This is normally to be considered imprudent, because these persons would have no knowledge of native customs, of the peculiar genius and mentality of the people, and of the language of the country. If such are to be appointed, they should first spend a few years in apostolic work among the people before taking up duties at the seminary.[7]

In the places of the missions it may be necessary to appoint one and the same person to several offices in the regional seminary. This can be done, especially if the number of students is as yet small. Thus the office of prefect of studies is usually filled by one of the professors, perhaps the most learned, or most experienced. The rector of the seminary could very well hold this office himself, as it is very compatible with the office of rector. The office of vice-rector may be held by one of the professors, a younger man who is with the students more than the others. Professors in service may be appointed the ordinary confessors for the students if the seminary is in charge of a religious institute or a society of priests,[8] as are the regional seminaries of China.

[6] *PCS*, n. 660.

[7] *Directorium*, nos. 260, 459.

[8] S. C. Sem. et Stud. Univ., 25 ian. 1928—*Enchiridion Clericorum*, n. 1247.

It is not necessary however that the two ordinary confessors belong to the seminary community,[9] and therefore missioners in nearby stations may be appointed the ordinary confessors, provided they can come to the seminary once a week, at least as a rule, for the fulfillment of their duties.[10] Whenever outsiders are appointed as the ordinary confessors, it would be advisable to have professors in the seminary designated as the extraordinary confessors, so that the seminarians actually have the opportunity to confess whenever they feel the need to do so.

Before leaving the subject of confessors, one may well ask whether or not they are to be appointed by the Superior General of the institute or by some other authority. It does not seem that confessors are really comprehended under the terms official, superior, moderator. They would therefore be appointed, not by the Superior General,[11] but by the rector of the seminary. The rector must of course choose such as are approved and have the faculties from the local Ordinary.[12]

The *spiritual director* must be distinct from the superiors of the seminary and must maintain residence within the walls of the institution.[13] Though the religious or missionary institute may find it difficult to supply a separate man for this position (since he cannot at the same time fill the office of even a lesser official), it must be remembered that the spiritual director carries on a work that is absolutely essential if the seminary is to fulfill its purpose and train holy and apostolic priests. Therefore, unless a competent priest can be found for this task, there is little reason for the seminary to exist. The spiritual director moreover can help in the teaching department of the seminary, taking such clas-

[9] Vermeersch—Creusen, *Epitome*, II, n. 692; Wernz—Vidal, *Ius Canonicum*, IV, ii, n. 696.

[10] Cf. can. 1367, 2°.

[11] Cf. *Normae* (1934), nos. 4, b, and 7 collated with n. 8—*Sylloge*, n. 183.

[12] Can. 874; *Directorium*, n. 533.

[13] *Normae* (1934), n. 8—*Sylloge*, n. 183.

ses as are duly compatible with his office, v.g., ascetic theology. If the seminary lacks a sufficient teaching personnel, he may teach even some of the auxiliary subjects, such as sacred eloquence, catechetics, sacred rites, etc., which demand less preparation than the primary disciplines.[14]

The *procurator* must be distinct from the rector,[15] for if the rector is concerned with the temporalities and the many details this administration involves, he will be impeded in the fulfillment of his own proper duties as the head of the seminary.

### *Professors*

In the appointment of professors for the regional seminary the Superior General will prefer those of his subjects who have obtained the doctorate or the licentiate in a university recognized by the Holy See, or who have a corresponding testimonial from the religious institute itself.[16] The common law does not demand that the professors have these degrees, but that those with degrees be preferred. Therefore the Superior General may appoint to professorships in the regional seminary priests who have not received degrees, provided however that they have the necessary learning. An exception obtains with reference to the professor of Sacred Scripture: he must have completed special courses of studies in that subject and have received at least the baccalaureate in Sacred Scripture before he may teach in the seminary.[17] In China, however, even this may not be possible, so that it will be licit to appoint to the professorship of Sacred Scripture one who has not received this degree—*ad impossibile enim nemo tenetur.*

Distinct professors are to be appointed at least in Sacred Scripture, dogma, moral theology, and ecclesiastical his-

[14] Brys, *Compendium,* II, n. 799; Vermeersch—Creusen, *Epitome,* II, n. 692.

[15] Can. 1358.

[16] Can. 1366, § 1; S. C.Sem. et Stud. Univ., 23 maii 1948—*AAS,* XL (1948), 260.

[17] Pius XI, motu proprio *Bibliorum scientiam,* 27 apr. 1924—*AAS,* XVI (1924), 180 sq.

tory.[18] Again, the requirement is of a relative rather than absolute character,[19] for although serious efforts must always be made for the achieving of the ideal, yet it will often take years of endeavor to attain it. In a regional seminary with courses in both philosophy and theology, the number of classes held in a week will be about 70 or 75, and if a preparatory year to philosophy is added, there will be 80 or 85 classes in a week.[20] For the carrying out of this program at least seven professors will be necessary, unless the number of students is very small. Usually the rector, spiritual director, and procurator will find it necessary to take over one or the other of the auxiliary subjects, and if that be so, they should choose subjects which are duly compatible with their offices.[21]

### Article 2. Rules of Discipline and Program of Studies

The institute to which the administration of the regional seminary is entrusted has the right and the duty to draw up the rules of discipline, the program of studies, the daily *horarium,* and the list of textbooks, all of which may be emended and must be approved by the Sacred Congregation for the Propagation of the Faith. When once approved, these items may not be changed without the consent of the same Congregation.[22] The Superior General of the institute will therefore appoint a commission to draw up these various statutes. The commission will consist of men well versed in scholastic philosophy and sacred theology, seminary administration and the peculiar needs of the mission lands.

The special statutes of the regional seminary may be

[18] Can. 1366, § 3.

[19] Vermeersch—Creusen, *Epitome,* II, n. 700; Coronata, *Institutiones,* II, n. 938, 6°; see also *PCS,* n. 660.

[20] Cf. "Ratio Studiorum Seminarii Regionalis de Fukien"—*Archivum S. C. P. F.,* Fu-chou, n. 3102/37 prot.; Cracco, *De Seminariorum Sinensium Institutione,* pp. 254-261; *Directorium,* n. 1268.

[21] *Directorium,* n. 1274, nota 83.

[22] *Normae* (1934), n. 3—*Sylloge,* n. 183.

modeled on the statutes successfully employed in other regional seminaries of the same country, and should incorporate, in precise and simple rules, the many instructions of the Holy See on the formation of the clergy, and the best recommendations given in the moral, canonical and ascetical works of those who have written on seminary life and administration.

It must be remembered that the regional seminary has for its purpose the formation of the secular and not the religious clergy, the rules of discipline being directed accordingly. For this reason the Superior General should consider it advisable to have the rules of discipline examined by the Ordinaries of the region, asking for suggestions and recommendations, before the rules are sent to the Sacred Congregation for its stamp of approval. The final redaction of the rules is of course the prerogative of the Superior General, and the definitive approval, the right of the Sacred Congregation.[23]

As to the subject matter of the special statutes of the seminary, the rules are to be made for the government both of the students and of those who are engaged in their training.[24] The rules for the superiors and professors may be entitled: "Norms for the Internal Administration of the Regional Seminary of N. in China." These norms enumerate the various officials of the seminary—rector, vice-rector, spiritual director, procurator, professors, prefect of studies—and delineate the duties assigned to each. These rules define the sphere of activity and authority of each official and call attention to pertinent provisions of the Code of Canon Law, to the instructions of the Sacred Congregation, and to the agreement between the institute and the Ordinaries of the region, as they affect each particular office and position.[25]

The rules of discipline for the students may be divided

[23] *Normae* (1934), n. 3—*Sylloge*, n. 183.

[24] Can. 1357, § 3.

[25] Cf. "Normae Generales Seminarii Regionalis de Fukien in Sinis" —*Archivum S. C. P. F.*, Fu-chou, n. 3102/37 prot.

into three convenient parts: exercises of piety, conduct towards others, and seminary regulations. The first part of the rules, exercises of piety, lists the various religious exercises or practices which are to be carried out daily, weekly, monthly and yearly. The essential practices are enumerated in canon 1367 of the Code, and to these should be added the ones suggested by decree 667 of the First Plenary Council of China. The rules of conduct cover the various relations of the seminarians with their superiors, professors, fellow-students, servants, and outsiders (guests, relatives etc.). Furthermore, the so-called "seminary regulations" comprise a wide variety of subjects: recreation, walks, vacations; visits from relatives; quality of garments; use of money; use of tobacco; requisite permission for various types of actions; assigned duties in and around the seminary; reasons for visiting one's home (sickness, death); and, finally, admission, expulsion, and sanctions.[26] To this there should be added the daily *horarium*, giving two distinct schedules—one for school days, the other for Sundays and Holydays. The changes to be made on the weekly free day (or two free afternoons) should be noted. A summer schedule may also be included, which will of course be pointed to relaxation rather than to serious application to study. These various orders of the day should aim to give a wise division of time to study, prayer, recreation and sleep.

It is certainly outside the scope of this dissertation to take up the various points of the rules of discipline in detail. Yet, in passing, one may commendably make special mention of the matter of vacations. For the rules of certain seminaries may easily be too strict on this important matter, shielding the students from the dangers of the world to such a degree

[26] "Regulae ab Alumnis Seminarii Regionalis S. Bonaventurae Servandae, Hankow"—*Coll. Comm. Syn.*, V (1932), pp. 736-744; "Regulae Seminarii Regionalis de Fukien"—*Archivum S. C. P. F.*, Fu-chou, n. 3102/37 prot; St. Charles Borromeo, *Institutiones—Acta Eccl. Med.*, III, 95-146; S. C. Ep. et Reg., *Norme per l'Ordinamento Educativo e Disciplinare dei Seminari d'Italia*, 18 ian. 1908 —*ASS*, XLI (1908), 212-242; *Directorium*, nos. 628-675, 806-899.

that more harm is done than good. The students are to be trained, not for the cloister, but for the apostolic life in the market place. If they are completely cut off from the world for seven years or even more, they may gain a conscious sense of certain difficulties only when it is too late to reconsider the form of life they have chosen. On the contrary, if they are allowed prudently to encounter the outside world each year, their spiritual formation will be more solid and they will learn gradually how to overcome the dangers to the priestly and apostolic life. There are not advocated long vacations in the parental home—short vacations at home are much more desirable. There are advocated longer vacations away from the seminary each year, but in the mission of one of the more experienced priests, or even better, in the central residence of the mission with the Bishop, where the seminarian may work as a catechist and gain useful experience in the work of the apostolate. This is in accord with the wish of the Fathers of the Synod of Ssu-ch'uan (Szechwan), who thought it proper to have the cleric spend a whole year in this work after the course of theology was completed, but before his promotion to the priesthood.[27]

### *The Program of Studies*[28]

The institute to which the seminary is committed has the right to draw up the program of studies, the distribution of

[27] Synod of Ssu-ch'uan, ch. VIII, n. 7—*Coll. Lacensis,* VI, 620. The *Directorium* has a complete discussion of the matter of vacations away from the seminary; see nos. 900-921.

[28] St. Charles Borromeo, *Institutiones,* Pars I—*Acta Eccl. Med.,* III, 95-116; S. C. Sem. et Stud. Univ., *Ordinamento dei Seminari,* 26 apr. 1920—*Enchiridion Clericorum,* nos. 1080-1116; S. C. Sem. et Stud. Univ., *Ordinationes,* 12 iun. 1931—*AAS,* XXIII (1931), 263-284; S. C. Sem. et Stud. Univ., *Normae . . . pro Pont. Seminariis Regionalibus Italiae,* 25 mart. 1936, Pars III—*Enchiridion Clericorum,* nos. 1419-1433; S. C. Ep. et Reg., *Programma generale Studiorum a Pio PP X approbatum pro omnibus Italiae Seminariis—ASS,* XL (1907), 336-343; "Ratio Studiorum Seminarii Regionalis de Fukien" —*Archivum S. C. P. F.,* Fu-chou, n. 3102/37 prot.; *Directorium,* nos. 1194-1289; Cracco, *De Seminariorum Sinensium Institutione,* pp. 170-194; Langasco, *De Institutione Clericorum in Disciplinis*

the courses, and the list of textbooks.[29] The institute has not the right to determine the studies to be taken in the seminary, since these are already determined by the law of the Code and various papal pronouncements.[30] The particulars of the study program will therefore contain the essential matters determined by the Code of Canon Law, and for the rest be based on the norms, preceptive and directive, of the papal decrees and instructions. All these norms should be applied to the conditions of the Chinese missions. The program should not be based too much on circumstances and present possibilities; rather, a more objective norm should be adopted and set up as the ideal to be eventually achieved. The ideal must however point to what is practicable and possible of eventual achievement.[31]

The *ratio studiorum* may be divided into the following parts: general rules; an enumeration of the courses; the distribution of the courses; examinations; a list of textbooks.

The general rules will cover the requirements to be met before a student will be admitted to the studies of philosophy and theology, and determine the length of the studies to be taken in the regional seminary. The time for the beginning and the end of the school year is determined, the number of school days in the year is set, and a list of free days and vacations is appended.

The enumeration of the courses and the distribution of the same will depend largely on the number of years devoted to the study of scholastic philosophy. While the two years are demanded, yet a third year is considered most useful. The third year may be a necessity in some seminaries in consequence of the inadequate training received in underdeveloped minor seminaries in the places of the missions. If this

*Inferioribus* (Romae: Typis Polyglottis Vaticanis, 1936), pp. 242-247.

29 *Normae* (1934)., n. 3, b—*Sylloge*, n. 183.

30 Cf. canons 1364-1365.

31 Cracco, *De Seminariorum Sinensium Institutione*, pp. 170-171.

is the case, the third year takes the form usually of a year preparatory to the study of philosophy. If a preparatory year is had, it will be devoted to the study of Latin, Chinese literature, the natural sciences, and perhaps one course in philosophy, preferably logic.[32]

The course in scholastic philosophy embraces (besides logic) criteriology, ontology, cosmology, psychology, theodicy, ethics, and history of philosophy. Besides these, there should also be courses in the kindred branches, namely apologetics, mathematics, physics, chemistry, biology, anthropology, civil history, languages, and education.[33] The course in sacred theology, which must last for four full scholastic years, includes dogmatic and moral theology, Sacred Scripture, ecclesiastical history, canon law, liturgy, sacred eloquence, ecclesiastical chant, pastoral theology, and catechetics.[34] To these may be added, either as separate courses or as parts of kindred disciplines, patrology, Christian archeology, Hebrew, and biblical Greek.[35]

The distribution of the courses will determine the number of hours to be devoted to the individual subjects each week, the number of semesters to be devoted to the individual disciplines, and the time spent in class and in study periods each day. The fundamental tracts in dogma, moral, Sacred Scripture, and canon law, ought to be given separately to the first class in theology. The other classes may be united, the courses being given in cycle. If possible, however, it would be good to have the fourth class separate from the others, so that the professors could devote more attention to the needs of those who will shortly exercise the sacred ministry. Some similar system of cycle courses may be used

[32] *Directorium*, n. 1200.

[33] Can. 1365, § 1; S. C. Sem. et Stud. Univ., 26 apr. 1920—*Enchiridion Clericorum*, n. 1100; 12 iun. 1931—*AAS*, XXIII (1931), 266-267; instr., 21 dec. 1944—*AAS*, XXXVII (1945), 173.

[34] Can. 1365, § § 2, 3.

[35] S. C. Sem. et Stud. Univ., 26 apr. 1920—*Enchiridion Clericorum*, n. 1106.

also in the study of philosophy, the first class however having the more fundamental tracts separately.

The schedule of courses ought to be so arranged that in each week there are between 20-25 classes of one hour each, including chant and sacred eloquence. The *horarium* should allow one hour or more of study for each hour of class. The school year ought to be arranged in such a manner that, with all the vacation and retreat days, the holidays, and the like, duly subtracted, there remain each year a solid 150 days on which the students are occupied for about 8½ or 9 hours in classes and study periods.[36]

The examinations are also given special mention in the program of studies. This section may also encourage and recommend various scholastic exercises, such as disputations, cases of conscience, "term" papers, etc. The rules however should determine exactly the time of the examinations, what note one requires to pass the tests, the examination of reparation on the part of those who have not been successful in the first test, and finally the advancement of the students from one class to the next.

The First Plenary Council of China demands that a general examination be held in major seminaries at least once a year.[37] For greater proficiency in study and with a view to the lessening of mental fatigue for the students, the examination as given but once a year on the entire year's work should be discouraged. The courses are so varied and numerous, and so demanding on the strength of the average student, that the system of a single examination each year is hardly conducive to a gradual and genuine progress in the mastery of the subjects. An examination after each semester is much more practical in the seminary studies, which are after all undergraduate, and once this examination is com-

[36] Cf. S. C. Sem. et Stud. Univ., *Normae . . . pro Pont. Seminariis Regionalibus Italiae*, 25 mart. 1936, III, nos. 3-6—*Enchiridion Clericorum*, nos. 1421-1424; Cracco, *De Seminariorum Sinensium Institutione*, pp. 182-184; *Directorium*, nos. 1266-1267.

[37] *PCS*, n. 670, 1°.

pleted the material ought not be included in the test at the end of the scholastic year. This, it is believed, serves the best interests of the students and gives substantial promise for their solid progress in study.[38]

The list of textbooks may be appended to the program of studies or may be drawn up as a separate document. It may be better to have the list separate from the program of studies, because the study program will ordinarily be of a more permanent character, whereas changes will be suggested in textbooks as new and more practical texts are published.[39]

In drawing up the list of textbooks (as well as in composing the program of studies) the religious or missionary institute may evade the excesses of opposing schools of thought by adhering strictly to the mind of the Church. The Church prescribes that the professors are to treat the studies of rational philosophy and sacred theology according to the method, doctrine, and principles of the Angelic Doctor,[40] and that consequently in philosophy and theology there are to be selected those textbooks which treat the material according to the doctrine of St. Thomas.[41] At the same time, the *ratio studiorum* should guarantee that genuine progress in science and lawful liberty in research be protected, for the Church wishes that, in matters in which there is a division of opinion among the best authors in Catholic schools, no one is to be forbidden to follow that opinion which seems to him to be nearer the truth.[42]

[38] For a more complete discussion of the matter, see Cracco, *De Seminariorum Sinensium Institutione,* pp. 180 sq.

[39] Permission of the Sacred Congregation for the Propagation of the Faith should be obtained for a change of textbook in the regional seminary. —Cf. *Normae* (1934), n. 3—*Sylloge,* n. 183.

[40] Can. 1366, § 2.

[41] Pius X, motu proprio *Doctoris Angelici,* 29 iun. 1914—*Fontes,* n. 701; S. C. Sem. et Stud. Univ., litt., 9 oct. 1921—*Enchiridion Clericorum,* n. 1134.

[42] Pius XI, litt. encycl. *Studiorum ducem,* 29 iun. 1923—*AAS,* XV (1923), 309, 323.

Finally, in drawing up the program of studies, one must remember that not all the courses called for by the instructions of the Holy See need be treated formally in their own proper classes distinct from other disciplines.[43] The essential notions of pastoral theology can be given in the courses in moral theology, canon law and liturgy; Christian archeology and biblical Greek can be treated in the course of Sacred Scripture; patrology, in ecclesiastical history, etc. Auxiliary courses are indeed to be given in the best possible manner, but the courses in the principal subjects should not be weakened in order that room may be made for formal and distinct classes in disciplines which cannot be regarded as essential.[44]

The program of studies must however provide for at least a two-year course of studies in philosophy and a four-year course in theology.[45] As is evident, this provision of the *Normae* does not differ from that of canon 1365 of the Code of Canon Law. As the Code determines a duration of study which is to be considered the minimum for the entire Latin Church,[46] number 2 of the *Normae* must be understood as simply applying this provision to regional seminaries in mission lands. The two-year course in philosophy and the four-year course in theology are therefore a basic requirement in clerical education, and it is not lawful to shorten, abbreviate, or accelerate the courses without the permission of the Holy See. The course in philosophy must extend over a time-period of 21 months (counting in the vacation at the end of the first year); the course in sacred theology must extend over a period of 45 months (again including the vacations after the first three years). To accelerate these courses by multiplying the number of classes held each week, or by

[43] Vermeersch—Creusen, *Epitome*, II, n. 699; Beste, *Introductio*, p. 666.

[44] Cf. Pius XII, sermo, 24 iun. 1939—*AAS*, XXXI (1939), 246.

[45] *Normae* (1934), n. 2—*Sylloge*, n. 183.

[46] S. C. Sem. et Stud. Univ., *Ordinamento dei Seminari*, 26 apr. 1920—*Enchiridion Clericorum*, n. 1099.

holding summer school, is contrary to the tenor of the law and the mind of the Holy See.[47]

It is laudable to extend the courses. This is especially the case in philosophy, where a three-year course is considered most desirable and, as has been mentioned above, even necessary if the students have not received an adequate preparation in the minor seminary.

### Article 3. The Agreement for the Economic Administration of the Regional Seminary

The regional seminary does not belong to the religious institute but to the Holy See. By its supreme authority the Holy See entrusts the entire administration of the seminary to a religious or missionary institute, which institute, through the rector and procurator of the seminary, has charge also of the seminary's property and funds. But since the regional seminary is erected for the purpose of serving the needs of the dioceses and missions of the region, the Holy See demands that the Superior General of the institute and the Ordinaries of the region enter into an agreement concerning the economic administration.[48] This agreement will determine just how and by whom the expenses of the seminary are to be met, will define the mutual obligations assumed by the contracting parties, and make particular rules for the administration of the funds.

A typical economic agreement should contain the following points:

1. The dioceses, province, or provinces for which the regional seminary is erected are named. The proprietorship of the seminary belongs to the Holy See, the government to the religious institute, the use to the Ordinaries of the dioceses or provinces. The legal representative before the civil government is determined.

2. The burden of support will be borne by the Ordinaries

[47] Can. 1365, § § 1, 2; S. C. de Religiosis, decl., 7 sept. 1909—*Fontes*, n. 4397; 31 maii 1910—*Fontes*, n. 4402.

[48] *Normae* (1934), n. 9—*Sylloge*, n. 183.

of the region, the religious institute assuming only the administration of the seminary's properties and funds.

3. The religious institute contracts no obligations as to debts already contracted, or to be contracted in the future. The ordinary expenses, not only of the students but also of the officials and professors, will be paid by the Ordinaries of the region. The assessments are *pro rata*, according to the number of students each diocese or mission has in the seminary. The institute however will receive no special remuneration for the services of the officials and professors, who will give their services gratuitously.[49]

4. The rector and procurator of the seminary may not make any extraordinary expenditures nor may they contract debts without the permission of the Ordinaries of the region.

5. In case of disagreement between the Ordinaries and the religious institute, the case is to be decided by the Sacred Congregation for the Propagation of the Faith.

6. This agreement may not be changed except upon a mutual consent given by the Ordinaries and the religious institute, and only with the permission of the Sacred Congregation for the Propagation of the Faith.[50]

Although the particulars of the economic agreement will vary for each individual seminary, ordinarily the religious institute does not oblige itself to contribute either for the erection of the seminary or for its functioning. The institute will be bound to answer to the Ordinaries of the region and to the Holy See for the spiritual, disciplinary and intellectual training of the students and for the administration of the seminary's funds. Each Ordinary will contribute towards the support of the seminary according to his means and ac-

[49] If remuneration is expected, it should be determined exactly in this agreement.

[50] Cf., v. g., "Conventio . . . inter Ordinarios Regionis Eccl. de Fukien et Ordinem Praedicatorum"—*Archivum S. C. P. F.*, Fu-chou, n. 3102/37 prot.; "Conventio Ordinariorum pro Seminario Regionali de Hongkong"—*Archivum S. C. P. F., Hsiang-kang* (Hongkong), n. 1299/27 prot.

cording to the provisions of the agreement, and the religious institute will serve the seminary without demanding material remuneration.

Actually the greater part of the funds for the ordinary expenses comes from the Pontifical Work of St. Peter the Apostle, which adopts single seminarians, or, more often, all the seminarians of a certain seminary *in globo*.[51] To establish a working capital for the seminary the Ordinaries of the region, or the religious institute,[52] or both, may through their benefactors attribute to the regional seminary mass foundations, burses of study, and life-annuity policies.[53] The annual income from these invested monies may serve to put the seminary on a more solid financial basis and make outside help less necessary. The money assigned as the endowment for a pious foundation must be carefully and profitably invested for the benfit of the foundation.[54] Since business of this kind requires more than ordinary prudence and ability, the matter may well be placed in the hands of the procurator of the mission in which the seminary is located, or entrusted to the care of the procurator of the religious institute in that country or province, for these men are usually more expert in these affairs.[55]

The agreement between the Ordinaries of the region and the Superior General of the religious or missionary institute should be submitted to the Sacred Congregation for the Propagation of the Faith for approval. This is not expressly stated in the *Normae* of 1934, but nevertheless seems to be obligatory. The *Norme* of 1921 state that an estimate of the seminary's income, an appraisal of the amount to be con-

[51] Cf. v.g., "Annua relatio Seminarii Regionalis de Tatung-Suiyüan, Sectio Philosophica (Suiyüan), 1 iul. 1940—30 iun. 1941"—*Archivum S.C.P.F.*, Sui-yüan, n. 5012/41 prot.; "Annua relatio Seminarii Regionalis de Hongkong, 1 aug. 1949—31 iul. 1950"—*Archivum S.C.P.F.*, Hsiang-kang (Hongkong), n. 4408/50 prot.

[52] Cf., v.g., *Statuta O.F.M.*, nos. 4 h, 91.

[53] Can. 1544.

[54] Can. 1547.

[55] *Directorium*, nos. 580-586.

tributed by the single missions, and an estimate of the funds necessary to operate the institution are to be submitted to the Sacred Congregation for approval.[56] A similar provision was contained in an earlier and provisory redaction of the *Normae* of 1934.[57] The final and definite draft of the *Normae* of 1934 omits this provision and in a general way calls for the economic agreement between the Ordinaries of the region and the religious institute. This might be interpreted as proof that the agreement need not be submitted to the Sacred Congregation for approval. But this may not be admitted. Since the entire administration of the seminary is subject to the supreme supervision of the Sacred Congregation for the Propagation of the Faith,[58] a matter as important as the economic agreement may not be withdrawn from the Congregation's direct influence. The agreement must therefore be approved by the Sacred Congregation.

### *Norme of 1921*

The *Norme* of 1921 have no corresponding title concerning the rights and duties of the religious institute, for seminaries erected and governed according to the provisions of these *Norme* are not entrusted to a religious institute. The rights and duties which the *Normae* of 1934 attribute to the Superior General of the institute, the *Norme* of 1921 give to the Ordinaries of the region. These matters are considered in other chapters of this dissertation.

[56] *Norme* (1921), 2 d—Part III (Documents), Document 3.

[57] "Normae pro Seminariis Regionalibus Quae Institutis Religiosis Regenda Concreduntur," n. 3, c—*Coll. Comm. Syn.* V (1932), 595.

[58] *Normae* (1934), n. 1—*Sylloge*, n. 183.

## CHAPTER VII

## RIGHTS AND DUTIES OF THE ORDINARIES OF THE REGION

Text

### III. De Iuribus et Officiis Ordinariorum Regionis

10. Ordinariis regionis cum suis alumnis colloqui et commercium epistolare habere licebit. Iisdem facultas erit libere ad Seminarium accedendi, lectionibus scholasticis quandoque adsistendi, periculis, disputationibus et praemiorum distributioni adstandi.

11. Promotio ad Sacros Ordines exclusivae competentiae est Ordinariorum singulorum alumnorum, quibus proinde tempestative a Rectore necessariae circa pietatem, scientiam coeterasque promovendorum qualitates informationes mittentur.

12. Ordinarii Regionis quotannis convenient ut de rebus Seminarii, videlicet de pietate, de disciplina, de studio, et de oeconomica administratione, accurate agant et examini subiiciant relationem circa haec a Rectore Seminarii conscriptam. Conventui praeerit Episcopus primus iuxta canonicas praecedentiae normas: Secretarii munere fungetur Ordinarius consecratione recentior. In hoc conventu singuli Ordinarii adprobabunt atque subsignabunt relationem annuam moralem et oeconomicam, iuxta hic adnexum schema redigendam atque ad Sacram Congregationem de Propaganda transmittendam.

13. Si quae sint animadversiones faciendae, hae generatim per Ordinarium loci Rectori communicentur.[1]

Translation

### III. Rights and Duties of the Ordinaries of the Region

10. The Ordinaries of the region may visit and correspond with their own students. They shall be

[1] *Normae* (1934), nos. 10-13—*Sylloge*, n. 183.

free to come to the seminary in order to assist now and then at the lectures, to attend examinations, scholastic disputations and the distribution of awards.

11. Promotion to sacred orders falls within the exclusive competence of the Ordinary of the individual students. The rector shall in good time send to the Ordinaries the necessary information regarding the piety, studies, and other qualities of those to be ordained.

12. The Ordinaries of the region shall meet every year to consider carefully all the matters relating to the discipline, piety, studies and economic administration of the seminary, and for this purpose they shall examine the written report presented by the rector of the seminary on these matters. The Bishop who is first according to the canonical rules of precedence shall preside at this meeting, the office of secretary being filled by the Ordinary most recently consecrated. At this meeting each of the Ordinaries shall approve and sign the annual spiritual and financial report of the seminary, which shall be drawn up according to the annexed outline, and forwarded to the Sacred Congregation for the Propagation of the Faith.

13. If any observations are to be made concerning the seminary, they are as a rule to be communicated to the rector of the seminary by the local Ordinary.

### ARTICLE 1. THE ORDINARY AND HIS STUDENTS

The *Normae* of 1934 grant to the Ordinaries the right to visit and to correspond with their own students. The Ordinaries are free to come to the seminary whenever they wish, in order to visit their clerics, to assist now and then at the lectures, to attend the examinations, scholastic disputations, graduation exercises and the like.[2] The personal visit of the Bishop with his students serves a manifold purpose. Since the students are away from their own dioceses for long periods of time, the visit of the Bishop may well serve to strengthen the bonds which unite the students to

[2] *Normae* (1934), n. 10—*Sylloge*, n. 183.

their proper diocese, the scene of their future apostolate. If the young clerics are forgotten by their own Superior they may ultimately become discouraged and alienated from the spirit of their own mission.[3] The visit makes it possible for the Bishop to know his subjects better, and frequent visits will be necessary if he wishes to obtain fuller knowledge of the dispositions, piety, ecclesiastical spirit and vocation of his students. Through information gained at such visits the Ordinary may assure himself that no one is promoted to Orders unless proof is at hand for his integrity of life and competent learning.[4]

The visit of the Bishop spoken of in number 10 of the *Normae* is not a canonical visitation but a simple visit with his students, the officials and professors, the evident purpose of which is to acquaint himself with the progress made by his students. The visit should also serve the purpose of acquainting the Ordinary with the general administration of the seminary, the observance of the rules of discipline, and the carrying out of the scholastic program. He is therefore invited to be present occasionally at the lectures, examinations and scholastic disputations. By prudent and well-timed visits of this kind the Ordinaries can keep watch over the scholastic and ecclesiastical training given in the regional seminary and prepare themselves to offer useful suggestions at the annual meeting of the Ordinaries of the region.[5] The Ordinaries must be mindful that at the time of their visits to the seminary they ought not to impose particular precepts on their students, or grant them special privileges the nature of which would be contrary to the general discipline of the seminary. They must be careful not to contradict in any way the authority of the rector of the seminary, lest the students lose respect for the officials, make light of their rules of discipline, and thus cause a disruption of ecclesiastical spirit and discipline in the seminary.[6]

[3] *Directorium*, n. 290. [4] Cf. can. 1357, § 2; *PCS*, n. 658, 4°.

[5] Cf. can. 1357, § 2; *Normae* (1934), n. 12—*Sylloge*, n. 183.

[6] Cracco, *De Seminariorum Sinensium Institutione*, pp. 27-28; *Directorium*, nos. 275, 290.

### *Ordinations*

The *Normae* state that promotion to sacred orders falls within the exclusive jurisdiction of the Ordinary of the individual students. The rector of the seminary is to send to the Ordinaries the necessary information regarding the piety, studies and other qualities of those to be ordained.[7]

The rector of the regional seminary therefore need send only such documents as are called for from the rector of a diocesan seminary, namely attestations as to the piety, learning and moral character of the one to be ordained. The Ordinary must see to it that all the provisions of the sacred canons are fulfilled, and it will be his duty to collect the other documents required before the candidate may be promoted to orders. For it is his obligation not to confer orders upon anyone unless he is morally certain from positive proofs that the candidate is canonically fit.[8]

In particular the documents to be forwarded by the rector of the seminary to the proper Ordinary are the following:

1. The petition of the candidate according to the provisions of canon 992 and the instruction *Quam ingens Ecclesiae* of the Sacred Congregation of the Sacraments.

2. A testimonial regarding the studies made as required for each of the orders by canon 976.[9]

3. A testimonial—the rector's own—regarding the candidate's piety, moral character and canonical fitness.[10]

4. If the retreat before orders is made at the regional seminary, a testimonial of the rector regarding the retreat made by the student as prescribed by canon 1001.[11]

5. If the Ordinary has delegated the rector of the seminary to receive the profession of faith, the oath against modernism, the oath to serve the missions, and the oath before ma-

[7] *Normae* (1934), n. 11—*Sylloge*, n. 183.

[8] Canons 973, § 3; 1357, § 2; *PCS*, n. 658, 4°.

[9] Can. 993, 2°.

[10] Can. 993, 3°; S. C. de Sacr., instr. *Quam ingens Ecclesiae*, 27 dec. 1930, § 2, n. 5—*AAS* XXIII (1931), 123.

[11] Can. 1001, § 4.

jor orders as prescribed by the Sacred Congregation of the Sacraments, the rector must also provide testimonials to the effect that these oaths have been taken and the profession of faith made.

6. If the Ordinary of a candidate delegates the rector of the seminary to give the examinations before orders as required by canon 996, the rector must also send testimonials to the effect that the examination has been held and the candidate has or has not passed the test.

The Ordinary of the candidate must provide for the following documents:

1. Testimonial letters of the local Ordinary in whose territory the candidate has dwelt long enough to contract a canonical impediment.[12]

2. Testimonial letters of the candidate's pastor which embody the results of the investigations made and of the publication of the name of the candidate.[13]

3. If a cleric is promoted to major orders *titulo missionis* the Ordinary must provide for his support,[14] and it is considered advisable to have the cleric sign an agreement concerning the type and amount of support to be given.[15]

4. If the Ordinary wishes to have his students ordained by another Bishop in a general ordination ceremony held at the regional seminary, he must send dimissorial letters to the ordaining Bishop or to the rector of the seminary who shall transmit them to the ordaining Bishop.[16]

Besides these various documents already mentioned, canon 993, 1°, calls for a testimonial of the last order received, or in case of first tonsure, of baptism and confirmation. In the case of ordinations performed by the candidate's own Ordinary it will not be necessary for the rector of the regional seminary to provide a testimonial of baptism and con-

[12] Can. 993, 4°. [13] Can. 1000, § 1.

[14] Can. 981, § 2; *PCS*, nos. 130, 370, 546-547.

[15] Gubbels, *Praxis Missionalis in Vicariatu Apostolico de Ichang* (Wuchang: the Franciscan Press, 1935), nos. 90-100 (hereafter cited *Praxis*).

[16] Cf. can. 956.

firmation, because the Ordinary must send these same testimonials to the regional seminary when the student seeks admission.[17] Nor will the rector be obliged to send a testimonial of the last order received, since the proper Ordinary will have a record of this ordination in his archives.[18] If on the other hand the candidate is to be ordained by a Bishop other than his proper Ordinary, it will be the duty of the proper Ordinary to send the testimonial required by canon 993, 1°, together with the dimissorial letters required by canon 955, § 1, since the *Normae* do not place this obligation on the rector of the regional seminary.[19]

That the Ordinary may assure himself of the canonical fitness of the candidate for orders, he may apply to the conditions of the missions the Instruction of the Sacred Congregation of Sacraments, *Quam ingens Ecclesiae*, 27 December, 1930.[20] This instruction does not seem to be obligatory in the territory subject to the Sacred Congregation for the Propagation of the Faith. Nevertheless it is most useful and should be applied by the Ordinaries of China for the best interests of the Church and of their own dioceses.[21]

Before first tonsure and the minor orders the candidate must present to the rector of the seminary a signed petition in which he signifies his intention to receive first tonsure and minor orders freely and of his own accord. The rector of the seminary adds to this petition his own opinion as to the canonical fitness of the candidate and sends both documents to the proper Ordinary. The Ordinary must then make a threefold investigation concerning the vocation, the moral character, and the canonical fitness of the candidate. This information is to be gathered from the officials and professors of the seminary, the pastor of the candidate and his

[17] Canon 1363, § 2.

[18] Can. 1010; cf. Bouscaren-Ellis, *Canon Law, A Text and Commentary* (Milwaukee: Bruce Publishing Co., 1946), p. 386 (hereafter cited *Canon Law*).

[19] Cf. *Normae* (1934), n. 11—*Sylloge*, n. 183.

[20] *AAS*, XXIII (1931), 120-129.

[21] *Directorium*, nos. 283, 1490.

family, and from a personal talk of the Bishop with the candidate.

Before the subdiaconate similar investigations shall be made. If a candidate is thereupon judged fit for sacred orders, he must sign a declaration confirmed by oath, that he approaches ordination freely and has knowledge of all the duties and obligations attached to sacred orders and has the sincere will to observe them.

Unless a very brief time intervenes from the reception of the subdiaconate, the same declaration is to be made again before the cleric is advanced to the diaconate and priesthood. New investigations will not ordinarily be necessary unless in the meantime circumstances arise which throw doubt on the candidate's vocation or his moral fitness to bear the burdens and fulfill the obligations imposed by sacred orders.[22]

After the documents have been collected and the investigations carried out, the law of the Code permits the candidate to be ordained, but only by his proper Bishop or with legitimate dimissorial letters from him.[23] With regard to the ordination of seculars the proper Bishop is the Bishop of the diocese in which the candidate for orders has a domicile together with origin, or a simple domicile without origin. In this latter case the candidate must confirm by oath his intention to remain in the diocese for life, unless he has already been incardinated into a diocese by first tonsure, or is ordained for the service of another diocese according to the provisions of canon 969, § 2, or is a professed religious who is ordained according to the provisions of canon 964, 4°.[24]

If the candidate is advanced to first tonsure by his own Bishop for the service of another diocese with the consent of the Bishop of that diocese, he is incardinated into that diocese according to canon 111, § 2.[25] The Bishop of the diocese

[22] S. C. de Sacr., instr. *Quam ingens Ecclesiae*, 27 dec. 1930—AAS XXIII (1931), 120-129.

[23] Can. 955.

[24] Can. 956.

[25] Pontificia Commissio ad Codicis Canones authentice Interpretandos (hereafter cited PCI), 24 iul. 1939—*AAS*, XXXI (1939), 321.

for whose service a layman has been advanced to first tonsure by his own Bishop has the exclusive right to confer orders on this cleric or to give dimissorial letters according to canon 955, § 1, even though the subject has not yet acquired a domicile in that diocese.[26]

Thus far it is simply the general law of the Code of Canon Law and its authentic interpretation of which an account has been taken. Special difficulties may arise with regard to the proper Bishop for the ordination of a student in the regional seminary. The candidates are of course preparing themselves for the diocese, vicariate or prefecture of the Ordinary who sent them to the seminary. The provisions of number 11 of the *Normae* seem more properly to refer to this Ordinary, at least in the matter of deciding whether or not the candidate is to be promoted to orders. It may well be that he is also the proper Bishop for conferring orders according to the provisions of canons 955 and 956. For the candidate for the first tonsure may not yet be 21 years of age, and his legal domicile together with origin or his simple domicile without origin may indeed be the diocese of the Bishop who sent him to the seminary.[27] This Bishop would then be the proper Bishop for promotion to first tonsure and the other orders.

If however the candidate for orders has no domicile, neither in the diocese of the Bishop who sent him to the seminary, nor in the diocese in which the seminary is located, nor elsewhere, the candidate must then either establish a domicile or obtain an apostolic indult to receive ordination. It seems beyond doubt that this seminarian could obtain his proper Bishop by establishing a domicile in the diocese of the Bishop who sent him to the seminary. This he could do during the time of the vacation he spends in the diocese for which he is studying. By the very fact that he goes to the diocese, takes the oath to remain there and to serve the diocese perpetually and therefore has indeed the intention to remain there for life, a domicile seems unquestionably ac-

[26] PCI, 24 iul. 1939—*AAS*, XXXI (1939), 321

[27] Canons 88, § 1; 90; 93, § 1; 956.

quired. The fact that the student almost immediately goes back to the regional seminary for his theological studies does not exclude the acquiring of a domicile in the diocese of his future labor. All the elements for acquiring a domicile seem to be present and the temporary absence for the purpose of study can certainly be reconciled with the intention of remaining perpetually in the diocese of adoption, unless something unforeseen calls him away from that diocese for good.[28]

Worthy of consideration here is a case argued before the Sacred Congregation of the Council. For in the arguments proposed by the Congregation for the solution of the case, one finds that in the opinion of the Congregation a student may obtain a domicile in the diocese for which he is studying by residence in the regional seminary which serves the diocese. The case was the following. Joseph, born in the diocese of N., left that diocese, and later entered a regional seminary located in the diocese of Y. Upon receiving dimissorial letters from the Bishop of the diocese X (a diocese served by the regional seminary of Y) he was promoted to the first tonsure and later to the minor and major orders including the priesthood. Still later, a disagreement having arisen between Joseph and the Bishop of X, Joseph claimed that he belonged to the diocese of his origin, N. The Sacred Congregation of the Council argued that Joseph had lost his domicile of origin in N, had acquired no new domicile, and was a *vagus* (Joseph had argued that he still had his domicile of origin). Since the Bishop of X was willing to take Joseph, and since the latter in fact received tonsure upon the Bishop of X's dimissorial letters, Joseph was incardinated into the diocese of X. The fact that he had no domicile there would at the most argue that canon 956 was violated, but it would not make the incardination invalid. Hence Joseph belonged to the diocese of X.

Important for us is what follows. The argument of the Congregation implied that in the case it seems that Joseph

[28] Beste, *Introductio*, p. 137; cf. also Vermeersch-Creusen, *Epitome*, I, n. 212, 3°.

did have a domicile after all, namely in the diocese of X. For the regional seminary is proper to all the dioceses it serves, and therefore seminarians who study in a regional seminary for one of the dioceses acquire a domicile in the particular diocese for which they are studying. The argument rests on an analogy with the legislation for public, or rather common, cemeteries. Every parish should have its own cemetery, unless the local Ordinary has legitimately designated one common cemetery for several parishes according to the provisions of canon 1208, § 1, and in this case each pastor retains the full rights over the common cemetery that he would enjoy in a cemetery proper to his parish. And so with the regional seminary, the Bishop for whose diocese the students are destined is competent to ordain them or issue dimissorial letters.[29]

Relying on this argument of the Sacred Congregation of the Council, the writer believes that a Bishop in China, when he has students over 21 years of age in a regional seminary, may consider these students as having a domicile in his diocese, and may therefore promote them to first tonsure and thus incardinate them into his diocese. Once incardinated into the diocese, there would be no further trouble, in-

[29] "Nec omittendum est quod in casu domicilium de iure non videtur defecisse: nam ex quo Iosephus, post inventum Episcopum benevolum receptorem X, in seminario regionali manere perrexit, perinde erat ac si in seminario dioecesano degisset: ita enim constituta sunt seminaria regionalia pro studiis philosophicis et theologicis in Italia, ut suppleant quod in singulis dioecesibus constituere seminarium dioecesanum iam non datur; argumento ducto ex analogia cum publicis coemeteriis in quae, ut notum est, singuli parochi suum ius integrum servant quod obtinebant in proprium cuiusque paroeciae coemeterium. Iure, itaque, nec ex errore, Episcopus X, in dimissorialibus pro diaconatu asserere potuit: 'Tibi R. D. subdiacono Iosepho, e territorio N. oriundo, nunc nostrae dioecesi legitime [nempe per susceptionem sacrae tonsurae] incardinato, facultatem facimus,' etc..."—S. C. Concilii, resolutio 10 mart. 1923—*AAS*, XVI (1924), 54. The argument certainly applies to regional seminaries in China as well as to those in Italy, since in China also the regional seminary supplies the lack of diocesan seminaries and is therefore proper to each diocese it serves.

asmuch as the Bishop of this diocese then exists as the proper Bishop for the conferring of the higher orders.

It may easily happen in China that the proper Ordinary for ordinations will be a Prefect Apostolic who is not a Bishop. This Ordinary may confer the first tonsure and the minor orders.[30] For promotion to major orders he may grant dimissorial letters to his subjects, so that they may be ordained by the Bishop of another mission.[31]

Since regional seminaries in China also provide for the philosophical and theological training of religious clerics, a word is in order regarding the ordination of these clerics. The ordination of non-exempt religious is governed by the law of secular candidates.[32] The local Ordinary of the diocese in which is located the religious house to which the religious candidates are attached will therefore either ordain these candidates or grant dimissorial letters so that they may be ordained by the Bishop of another diocese, provided that the candidates are in perpetual vows. If there is question of the advancement of a religious in temporary vows to first tonsure and minor orders, since the religious did not lose the proper diocese which he had in secular life,[33] the Bishop of the diocese where the religious had a domicile before he entered the community remains his proper Bishop in the matter of ordination. This Bishop shall therefore have the authority to ordain or to issue dimissorial letters.[34]

Exempt religious receive dimissorial letters from their own major superiors.[35] The Bishop to whom the clerics

[30] Can. 957, § 2.

[31] Can. 958, § 1, 4°.

[32] Can. 964, 4°.

[33] Cf. can. 585.

[34] Woywod, *A Practical Commentary on the Code of Canon Law* (9th printing, revised by Callistus Smith, 2 vols., Now York: Joseph F. Wagner, 1945), I, nos. 903-904 (hereafter cited *Practical Commentary*). It may be noted that many Missionary Institutes have the privilege to grant dimissorials to their subjects so that they may be ordained by the local Ordinary, or in some cases, by any Ordinary in communion with the Holy See.

[35] Can. 964, 2°.

should be sent for ordination is the Bishop of the diocese in which is located the religious house to which the clerics belong. This Bishop may grant permission that the clerics be ordained by some other Bishop.[36] An Abbot actually holding office may himself confer first tonsure and minor orders, and if he is a titular Bishop he may also confer major orders on his own subjects.[37]

### *Admission to the Seminary*

It is the right of each Ordinary of the region to send his students in philosophy and theology to the regional seminary, and admission to the seminary depends on the single Ordinaries.[38] The statutes of the regional seminary are to be observed in this matter, lest there be admitted such as are not prepared for the studies to be undertaken.

When an Ordinary wishes to send a student to the seminary he should send to the rector of the seminary a certificate of baptism and confirmation, and testimonial letters asserting the legitimate birth, the good moral character of the student, and a testimonial of the studies already successfully undertaken.[39] Since students of many minor seminaries are sent to the same regional major seminary, a real difficulty arises regarding the degree of learning attained by the various students. It is evidently desirable that the students of the various dioceses attain approximately the same degree of learning in Latin and in the ecclesiastical and the profane sciences in their own minor seminaries. The regional seminary can function smoothly only if the students are well prepared for the studies to be taken. In order to obviate difficulties in this matter, Archbishop Celso Constantini, Apostolic Delegate in China, proposed three methods to be employed. An examination before admission to the

[36] Canons 965-966.

[37] Can. 964, 1°, collated with can. 959; cf. Woywod, *Practical Commentary,* I, n. 901.

[38] *Normae* (1934), n. 5—*Sylloge,* n. 183; canons 1354, § 3; 1363, § 1; *PCS,* n. 651.

[39] Can. 1363, § 2; *PCS,* n. 655.

regional seminary, or a preparatory year in the regional seminary, or a common program of studies in all the minor seminaries served by the regional seminary.[40]

Of the methods suggested the first seems to be the least acceptable. For either the entrance examination will be enforced strictly, or it will become a mere formality. If enforced strictly, it will indeed benefit the seminary, but it will not solve the problems of the students rejected. If not enforced strictly, the difficulty will remain as before, much to the discomfiture of the professors of the seminary.

The second plan is practical for it takes nothing for granted. The regional seminary itself devotes an entire year to the preparation of the students for the more arduous studies in philosophy and theology. The documents consulted in regard to the establishment of the 15 regional seminaries in China reveal that this plan was adopted, at least in the beginning, by several of the seminaries.

The third method suggested by the Apostolic Delegate is by far the best. It calls for a long-range program which assures a fixed standard of education for all aspirants to the regional seminary. This plan was adopted by the Ordinaries of the ecclesiastical regions of Hu-pei and Hu-nan in 1932. The rectors of the minor seminaries of the two regions met in Han-k'ou in July, 1932, to treat of this very matter. The meeting was presided over by Bishop Eugenio Massi, O.F.M., the Vicar Apostolic of Han-k'ou and for this meeting the delegate of the other Ordinaries of the two regions of Hu-pei and Hu-nan. In the meeting, the rectors of the minor seminaries adopted a uniform program of studies, a uniform list of textbooks and a uniform rule of discipline for all the minor seminaries of the ecclesiastical regions of Hu-pei and Hu-nan. The students of these regions pursue their philosophical and theological studies at the Regional Seminary of Han-k'ou.[41] One may with reason take exception to par-

[40] Letter of Archbishop Constantini, 28 August, 1932—*Coll. Comm. Syn.*, V (1932), p. 917.

[41] "De Seminario Minore"—*Coll. Comm. Syn.*, V (1932), pp. 1137-1152.

ticular provisions of this agreement, but taken as a whole it is an admirable plan for the purpose intended—the uniform preparation of the students for their studies in the regional major seminary.

### *Dismissal from the Seminary*

The *Normae* give us no information regarding the dismissal of students from the regional seminary. The special rules of discipline of the regional seminary may treat of the matter, or the individual Ordinaries may have some agreement on the matter with the officials of the seminary. If no special provisions exist, it would remain the prerogative of the Ordinaries to dismiss their own students.

The Code of Canon Law states that troublemakers, the incorrigible, the rebellious, those who do not seem suited to the ecclesiastical state, should be dismissed; also those who make so little progress in studies that there is no hope that they will ever acquire sufficient learning; but especially should those be immediately dismissed who have failed against good morals or against the faith.[42]

The Code distinguishes between simple dismissal and expulsion. The causes for dismissal are numerous and varied, and the dismissal would take place after a sufficient probation and by the common method, namely, the decision of the Ordinary of the student. In these cases the Ordinary will of necessity be guided by the opinion and advice of the rector and officials, who are in a position to know better than he whether or not a student should be dismissed.[43]

The causes for outright expulsion are grave lapses against good morals or against the faith, which must of course be known and established facts in the external forum before the authorities may proceed to the expulsion of the student. In these cases the student is to be expelled immediately without time for emendation,[44] and, so it seems, by the rector of

[42] Can. 1371.

[43] Cracco, *De Seminariorum Sinensium Institutione*, p. 112; *Directorium*, n. 280.

[44] Can. 1371.

the seminary on his own authority if there is question of grave scandal or imminent danger of perversion. In order to preclude dangerous delays in these matters the Ordinaries of the region should grant to the rector of the regional seminary sufficiently broad faculties to let him act promptly and efficiently in all cases. In granting these faculties the Ordinaries may append the condition of a definitive or consultive vote of the other officials and professors, and demand that they be notified of the causes and results of the case as soon as possible.[45]

Great prudence is called for in the dismissing of a student if the least possible harm is to come to the student and his family. The young man should be aided by way of considerate treatment, good advice, and recommendations for a position in the world if possible. This spirit of charity will make it easier for the unfit and unworthy to leave the seminary, and at the same time will make friends for religion, allay grudges, and prevent enmities between the dismissed and the Bishop.[46]

## Article 2. The Ordinaries and the Administration of the Seminary

The Ordinaries of the region must take a great interest in the administration of the regional seminary. For in this institution are trained the priests who constitute the hope of the Church in their dioceses. The first duty of the Ordinaries is to form a native clergy so well trained and educated that the native priests are able to fill every ecclesiastical office, even that of governing the missions. Since it is impossible for the Ordinaries to have diocesan major seminaries to carry out this work, the proper management of the regional seminary must become for them a matter of intimate concern that demands their serious and constant attention.[47]

[45] *Directorium*, nos. 280-281, 291; Cracco, *De Seminariorum Sinensium Institutione*, pp. 112-113; Coronata, *Institutiones*, II, n. 943.

[46] Cf. Coronata, *Institutiones*, II, n. 943.

[47] S. C. P. F., instr., 23 nov. 1845; instr., 19 oct. 1883—*Fontes*, nos. 4816; 4903; Pius XI, litt. encycl. *Rerum Ecclesiae*, 28 febr.

In particular the various duties of the Ordinaries in regard to the administration of the seminary may be enumerated as follows:

Before the seminary is constituted a *regional* seminary, the Ordinaries must enter into an agreement with the Superior General of the religious or missionary institute concerning the economic administration of the seminary.[48] Once the agreement is made, the Ordinaries must fulfill their own part as a matter of justice toward the religious institute which has assumed the burden of administration.

Promotion to orders is the exclusive right and duty of the respective Ordinary.[49]

The Ordinaries should visit the seminary frequently in order to acquaint themselves with the progress of their own students, the observance of the rules of discipline, and the functioning of the scholastic program.[50]

The Ordinaries are to meet each year to consider and discuss the state of discipline, piety, studies and economic administration. At this meeting the written report of the rector is to be examined, approved and signed, and forwarded to the Sacred Congregation for the Propagation of the Faith. If any observations are to be made, they shall be communicated to the rector of the seminary by the local Ordinary.[51]

The Ordinaries should not raise difficulties if a priest of their diocese is nominated to an office or professorship in the seminary. They ought rather to have some of their priests undertake higher studies in the ecclesiastical sciences, so that their priests are prepared to fill such offices should the Superior General nominate or appoint them.[52]

1926—*AAS*, XVIII (1926), 65-83; litt. apost. *Officiorum omnium*, 1 aug. 1922— *AAS*, XIV (1922), 449-458.

[48] *Normae* (1934), n. 9—*Sylloge*, n. 183.

[49] *Normae* (1934), n. 11—*Sylloge*, n. 183.

[50] Cf. *Normae* (1934), n. 10—*Sylloge*, n. 183.

[51] *Normae* (1934), nos. 12-13—*Sylloge*, n. 183.

[52] Cf. Pius XI, litt. encycl. *Ad catholici sacerdotii*, 20 dec. 1935—*AAS*, XXVIII (1936), 37-52; *Enchiridion Clericorum*, n. 1383.

## *The Meeting of the Bishops*

Of the duties imposed by the *Normae* only the meeting of the Bishops has not yet been treated.

The subject-matter of the meeting.

The meeting of the Ordinaries is to be held each year, the subject-matter of the meeting being determined by number 12 of the *Normae* and the outline of the annual report. The following matters are to be discussed:

1. Piety. Are the spiritual exercises prescribed by the rules of discipline carried out faithfully?

2. Discipline and moral training. Do the officials of the seminary insist on a strict yet reasonable observance of the rules of discipline? Are confessors in a sufficient number appointed for the students? Are conferences on the ascetic and apostolic life given by the spiritual director? Does the spiritual director have the confidence of the students? Does the seminary maintain a truly ecclesiastical atmosphere?[53]

3. Studies. Do the officials and professors observe the program of studies, and use the textbooks approved for the seminary by the Sacred Congregation for the Propagation of the Faith? Are the professors competent in their fields of learning? Are the examinations well worked out and properly given, so that students are not merely pushed along from one class to another regardless of any deficient acquisition of solid learning?

4. Economic administration. Have the provisions of the common law, the instructions of the Holy See, and the agreement between the Ordinaries and the religious institute been faithfully observed in the administration of the temporal goods of the seminary?

5. Miscellanea. Other matters of discussion may appear in the examination of the annual report. Examples of such matters are: the reasons for the expulsion of a student, the problems of the students who have not advanced to the next class because they failed in the examinations, the living

[53] Cf. *Directorium,* n. 277, 4°.

conditions of the seminary, the facilities at hand for proper relaxation. The Ordinaries may also wish to consider a uniform set of regulations for those students who are called home during vacation periods to take part in liturgical services, the work of catechising, etc.[54] By treating all the clerics alike, the several Ordinaries can effectively forestall the occasion for dissentions and jealousies among them.[55]

The Ordinaries, it must be noted, are not competent to change the rules of discipline, the exercises of piety, the program of studies, the textbooks, nor can they dismiss officials and professors. The right and duty of the Ordinaries is to insist that the program of the seminary be carried out efficiently and properly. When cases of grave abuse or incompetence are discovered, the Ordinaries should report the same to the Sacred Congregation for the Propagation of the Faith.

The Time of the Meeting.

The time of the meeting is not determined by the *Normae*. However, since the annual report is to be sent to the Sacred Congregation for the Propagation of the Faith before 31 December of each year,[56] the meeting could well be held in September, October or November. This arrangement gives the rector ample time to draw up the report for the preceding scholastic year, and allows a sufficient period of time for the report to reach Rome before the end of December. The meeting may, by agreement of the Ordinaries, be set once and for all to coincide with the beginning of the new scholastic year.

The officers of the meeting.

The *Normae* determine that the Bishop who is first according to the canonical rules of precedence shall preside

[54] Synod of Ssu-ch'uan (Szechwan), chapter VIII, n. 7— *Collectio Lacensis*, VI, 618-620.

[55] *Directorium*, n. 295.

[56] *Normae* (1934), allegatum—*Sylloge*, n. 183.

over the meeting, the office of secretary being filled by the Ordinary most recently consecrated.[57]

Since the meeting will usually be held at the regional seminary itself, the presiding officer will be the Metropolitan of the province in which the seminary is located, provided that the Metropolitan belongs to the body of Bishops who send their students to the regional seminary. Otherwise he would not be present at the meeting. If the Metropolitan of the province is not present at the meeting, the local Ordinary will preside, inasmuch as he is given precedence over the other Bishops by the Code of Canon Law. This would be the case even though the Archbishop of another province is present.[58] By way of courtesy however the local Ordinary may yield his place of honor to the Archbishop of another province.[59]

The office of secretary is filled by the Ordinary most recently consecrated. This provision of the *Normae* is consonent with the tradition of ecclesiastics to have the junior member of a board serve as secretary. The terminology of the Latin text of the *Normae* seems inexact. According to the original Italian text: "Presiederà il Vescovo a cui spetta la precedenza secondo le norme canoniche; fungerà da Segretario l'Ordinario di nomina più recente."[60] The secretary is therefore the Ordinary most recently promoted to the episcopate, not the Ordinary most recently consecrated Bishop. This is more in conformity with canon 106, which states that if several persons stand in the same degree of rank and orders, they take precedence in the order of time in which they were elevated to rank. If they were promoted to the same degree of rank at the same time, then seniority in the

[57] *Normae* (1934), n. 12—*Sylloge*, n. 183.

[58] *Normae* (1934), n. 12; -canons 280, 347.

[59] Cf. S.R. C., 26 nov. 1919, ad V, n. 3—*AAS*, XII (1920), 178.

[60] "Norme per i Seminari Regionali Affidati ad Instituti Religiosi o Missionari (approvate con rescritto della Sacra Congregazione di Propaganda Fide, 27 aprile 1934)," n. 12—*Archivum S. C. P. F.*, n. 1989/34 prot., rub. 71/3.

reception of orders determines precedence.[61] If one of the Ordinaries at the meeting is a Prefect Apostolic who has not been elevated to the episcopate, the canonical norms of precedence ought to be applied, so that in this case the Prefect Apostolic would serve as secretary since he stands lowest in the order of precedence.[62]

The annual report.

The annual report, approved and signed by the Ordinaries is to be sent to the Sacred Congregation for the Propagation of the Faith. The *Normae* do not determine the person whose duty it will be to dispatch this report to Rome. Since the *Normae* do not place this obligation on the rector of the seminary, but merely demand that he present the report to the board of Ordinaries,[63] it seems to be the duty of the secretary of the meeting to dispatch the report to Rome by the authority of the board of Ordinaries.

Observations to be made.

As a result of the meeting, the Ordinaries may feel that it is their duty to make various observations regarding the discipline, studies, piety and economic status of the seminary. If such be the case, these observations are to be communicated to the rector of the seminary by the local Ordinary.[64] If it is judged opportune, letters may be sent to the Superior General of the religious or missionary institute to which the seminary is committed and also to the Sacred Congregation for the Propagation of the Faith.[65]

Number 13 of the *Normae,* which provides for observations to be made to the rector of the seminary through the local Ordinary, seems to refer only to such comments as are the result of the annual meeting, or as are made at another time but in the name of the board of Bishops. Should an in-

[61] Can. 106, 3°.

[62] Persons of the same rank but of a different order have precedence according to the higher or lower order. —Cf. can. 106, 3°.

[63] *Normae* (1934), n. 15—*Sylloge,* n. 183.

[64] *Normae* (1934), n. 13—*Sylloge,* n. 183.

[65] *Directorium,* n. 296.

dividual Ordinary have any recommendations, complaints or comments to make at any other time, there is no reason to demand that these be presented to the rector by the local Ordinary.

### *Résume*

The jurisdiction of the Ordinaries over the regional seminary is very limited. The regional seminary is in law not an institution or property of the diocese or the province in which it is located, but of the Holy See itself. Supreme jurisdiction over the regional seminary in mission lands is held and exercised by the Sacred Congregation for the Propagation of the Faith. The Congregation approves the rules of discipline and the program of studies, appoints the rector and has authority to ratify the choice of officials and professors. Without the permission of this Congregation students of the region served by the regional seminary are not allowed to study elsewhere than at the regional seminary.[66] The Sacred Congregation commits the execution of this program to a religious or missionary institute, giving to the institute almost complete control of the daily life at the seminary, and of the ordinary administration of the seminary itself.[67] The Ordinaries have not the right to appoint officials and professors; they do not prescribe the rules of discipline and the program of studies; nor do they approve the list of textbooks. They cannot remove or change the officials or professors.[68]

The rights of the Ordinaries over their own students are described in numbers 10 and 11 of the *Normae* and have been commented on above.[69] The rights of the Ordinaries over the administration of the seminary are delineated in numbers 12 and 13 of the *Normae* and consist of the faculty to examine and approve the annual report of the seminary, to inquire into the state of piety, learning, discipline and fi-

[66] *Normae* (1934), nos. 1, 3, 4, 5—*Sylloge*, n. 183.

[67] *Normae* (1934), nos. 1, 3, 4b, 7, 14, 16.

[68] *Normae* (1934), nos. 3, 4.

[69] Cf. Chapter VII, article 1, The Ordinary and His Students.

nance in the seminary, and to make known their observations on these matters to the rector of the seminary.

The Ordinaries have the obligation of vigilance over the seminary. If they discover that the rules of discipline are not observed, that the decrees of the Holy See are not enforced, that the professors are incompetent, that the funds are squandered and dissipated, etc., they most certainly have the obligation to report such abuses to the Sacred Congregation for the Propagation of the Faith, whose duty it is to take effective measures to correct them.[70]

## ARTICLE 3. DIFFERENCES IN THE *Norme* OF 1921

The rights and duties of the Ordinaries of the region are much more extensive when the regional seminary is entrusted, not to a religious or missionary institute, but to the secular clergy. The Ordinaries then have the actual administration of the seminary in their own hands, under the supreme direction of the Sacred Congregation for the Propagation of the Faith.[71]

The *Norme* of 1921 give the following powers to the Ordinaries of the region:

The right to choose the location of the seminary.

The right to draw up the rules of discipline, the program of studies and the list of textbooks.

The right to appoint and dismiss professors.

The right to present a candidate for the office of rector.

The right to appoint and dismiss the spiritual director, the procurator and other officials, the rector excepted.[72]

The choice of location, the rules of discipline, the program of studies, the textbooks, the appointment and dismissal of professors, must all however be approved by the Sacred

[70] Cf. *Directorium*, nos. 296, 309.

The special jurisdiction of the local Ordinary over the seminary is discussed in Chapter VIII, article 2.

[71] The *Praxis* of the Congregation no longer favors this system. Regional seminaries in mission lands are as a rule entrusted to a religious or missionary institute according to the *Normae* of 1934.

[72] *Norme* (1921), nos. 2, 3, 7—Part III (Documents), Document 3.

Congregation for the Propagation of the Faith. The rector is appointed by the Sacred Congregation. The other officials are appointed by the Ordinaries with the advice of the rector, and no approval is required.[73]

The Ordinaries of the region have ordinary jurisdiction over the regional seminary, but must exercise it through the Ordinary of the mission in which the seminary is located. The local Ordinary has the exclusive right of vigilance over the discipline, the scholastic program and the entire administration of the seminary. It is also his right and duty to put into execution the resolutions agreed upon in the annual meeting of the Ordinaries.[74]

In common with the *Normae* of 1934 the *Norme* of 1921 call for the annual meeting of the Ordinaries to discuss the discipline, studies and economic administration of the seminary. The presiding officer and the secretary of the meeting are determined in practically the same way as in the *Normae* of 1934. The rules for ordinations are for all practical purposes the same in both sets of norms.[75]

In drawing up the rules of discipline, the program of studies and the details of the financial administration of the seminary the Ordinaries may with profit consult the various instructions of the Holy See, made both before and after the Code of Canon Law, and intended for the seminaries of Italy. The more recent and important pre-Code documents are:

1. S.C.Ep.et Reg., Norme per l'Ordinamento Educativo e Disciplinare dei Seminari d'Italia, 18 ian. 1908.[76]

2. S.C.Ep.et Reg., Programma Generale Studiorum a Pio PP. X Approbatum pro Omnibus Italiae Seminariis, 10 maii, 1907.[77]

[73] *Norme* (1921), nos. 2, 3, 7—Part III (Documents), Document 3.

[74] *Norme* (1921), nos. 5, 9— Part III (Documents), Document 3.

[75] Cf. *Norme* (1921), nos. 6, 8—Part III (Documents), Document 3.

[76] Italian text: *ASS*, XLI (1908), 212-242. Latin text: Micheletti, *Ius Pianum* (Augustae Taurinorum: Marietti, 1914), pp. 767 sq.

[77] Italian text: *ASS*, XL (1907), 336-343. Latin text: Micheletti, *Ius Pianum* p. 766. 767.

The more important documents after the Code of Canon Law are:

1. S.C.de Sem. et Stud. Univ., Ordinamento dei Seminari, 26 aprile, 1920.[78]

2. S.C.de Sem. et Stud. Univ., Normae statutae pro Pont. Seminariis Regionalibus Italiae, 25 mart. 1936.[79]

These documents, for varied and obvious reasons, can serve merely as directive norms for the Ordinaries of the Chinese missions who are subject to the Sacred Congregation for the Propagation of the Faith. In applying the contents of these instructions to the administrative, scholastic and disciplinary program of regional seminaries in China which are entrusted to the secular clergy, these Ordinaries cannot undertake anything that would prove derogatory to the *Norme* of 1921.

[78] *Enchiridion Clericorum,* nos. 1080-1116.
[79] *Enchiridion Clericorum,* nos. 1400-1433.

# CHAPTER VIII

## RIGHTS AND DUTIES OF THE RECTOR

Text

IV. De Iuribus et Officiis Rectoris Seminarii

14. Rector est Superior immediatus Seminarii eique coeteri moderatores et magistri parebunt.

15. Quotannis, quin personaliter ordinarie intersit, Episcoporum Conventui exactam relationem de statu morali et oeconomico Seminarii submittet.

16. Seminarium cum suis adiacentiis a iurisdictione paroeciali loci eximitur; officia paroecialia naturae pii instituti consentanea Rectori tribuuntur, qui relate ad confessiones alumnorum se gerat ad mentem canonis 518, § 2, C.I.C.[1]

Translation

IV. Rights and Duties of the Rector of the Seminary

14. The Rector is the immediate superior of the seminary, and the other officials and professors are his subordinates.

15. Each year, but without ordinarily being personally present, he shall submit to the meeting of the Bishops an accurate report of the moral and economic status of the seminary.

16. The seminary with its adjacent property is exempt from the jurisdiction of the local pastor; the parochial duties compatible with the nature of a pious institute belong to the Rector of the seminary, who in regard to the confessions of the students shall observe the spirit of canon 518, § 2, of the Code of Canon Law.

### Article 1. The Office of Rector

The rector of the regional seminary will in general have the same rights and duties as the rector of the diocesan seminary. Yet the nature of the regional seminary together with its particular rules and norms of government

[1] *Normae* (1934)—*Sylloge*, n. 183.

will demand various modifications in some important matters; thus the dependence of the rector of the diocesan seminary on the local Ordinary is complete according to the provisions of canon 1357, § 1, whereas the rector of the regional seminary is hardly dependent on the local Ordinary at all. The principal rights and duties which the rector of the regional seminary has in common with the rector of the diocesan seminary may be enumerated as follows.

1. He must make the profession of faith called for by canon 1406, § 1, but need not take the oath against modernism unless he is also one of the professors of the seminary.[2]

2. All must obey the rector in the fulfillment of their respective duties.[3] Since the rector is the head of the seminary, the entire internal administration is in his hands, and it is his right and duty to see to the proper moral, scholastic and material management of the institution. The other officials are to be his aides in carrying out the program of discipline, piety, studies and financial administration. All the personnel must therefore be immediately subject to him in those things which pertain to the life of the seminary.[4]

3. The rector of the seminary must see to it that the rules of discipline are observed. He must insist that the program of studies is followed and that the various disciplines are imparted according to the many directives of the Holy See regarding the studies to be made in philosophy and theology. For this reason the rector should visit the classes and be particularly regular in attending the examinations. He must see to it that the students are imbued with a truly ecclesiastical spirit. The exercises of piety called for by canon 1367 and by the rules of discipline of the seminary must be carried out properly. Since the rector of the seminary is the representative of ecclesiastical authority in the seminary,

[2] Genicot-Salsmans, *Institutiones Theologiae Moralis* (16. ed., 2 vols., Bruxellis: Dewit, 1946), I, n. 197 bis, in nota 1.

[3] Can. 1360, § 2.

[4] Cf. S. C. Ep. et Reg. *Norme per l'Ordinamento Educativo e Disciplinare dei Seminari d' Italia,* 19 ian. 1908, arts. 22-26—apud Micheletti, *Ius Pianum,* 769.

it will be his duty to watch over these exercises to safeguard them against possible neglect.[5]

4. The students must be instructed in the rules of Christian urbanity and etiquette. They must be taught to observe the rules of personal hygiene, to attend to cleanliness of person and apparel, and to cultivate a certain affability together with modesty and reserve in their relations with others.[6]

5. The rector should carefully watch that the professors do their work well.[7] He should be ready to consult with the professors and officials regarding the progress of study, the increase of piety, and the consolidation of discipline in the seminary, and give these same professors and officials ample opportunity and freedom to carry out their assignments without repeated interference.

6. Regarding the financial administration, it is stated that the procurator should be distinct from the rector.[8] Nevertheless, since the rector is the immediate superior of the seminary, it is his duty to keep informed about the financial status of the institution and also to see to it that the provisions of law are carried out in the handling of the funds.[9] With regard to the benefactors, the rector ought to inform them not to add onerous conditions in the founding of burses or the giving of alms. And in order to forestall various difficulties and troubles, the students are as a rule not to be allowed to write to their benefactors, but all business of this kind should be carried on between the rector and the benefactors without the knowledge of the students.[10]

7. Except for matrimonial matters, and strictly within the restrictions set by canon 891 with reference to the hearing

[5] Canons 1367; 1369, § 1; Onclin, "De Rectoribus Seminariorum," *Jus Pontificium* (Romae, 1921-1940), XV (1935), 293-294.

[6] Can. 1369, § 2; *PCS*, n. 668, 2°.

[7] Can. 1369, § 3.

[8] Can. 1358.

[9] Onclin, "De Rectoribus Seminariorum," *Jus Pontificium*, XV (1935), 295-296.

[10] *PCS*, n. 678.

of confessions, the office of pastor for all persons in the seminary is filled by the rector of the seminary and his delegate.[11] The essence of canon 1368 is incorporated into the *Normae,* but it must be noted that number 16 of the *Normae* provides that the rector of the regional seminary conduct himself according to the tenor of canon 518, § 2, with regard to the confessions made by the students.

8. The dismissal of the students has been considered in Chapter VII.

*Particular Duties of the Rector of the Regional Seminary*

Besides these duties which are common to the rectors of all seminaries, the rector of the regional seminary also has duties which are peculiar to his office. Most of these refer to his obligations toward the Ordinaries of the region served by the seminary, and have been considered in Chapter VII. The rector may also adopt a provision of the *Norme* of 1921 as a matter of practical policy. Namely he may periodically send a report to the individual Ordinaries regarding the progress in piety and learning made by their respective students.[12] The making of some such report seems obligatory. It serves the purpose of informing the Ordinaries regarding thc capabilities and dispositions of their students. Reports of this kind kept up for a number of years will be of great value to the Ordinaries when faced with the need of deciding whether or not a student should be promoted to orders.

With regard to the economic administration, it will be the duty of the rector of the seminary to observe the provisions of the agreement between the Ordinaries of the region and the Superior General of the religious or missionary institute to which the seminary has been entrusted.[13] The rector and the procurator must therefore administer the funds accord-

[11] Can. 1368.

[12] *Norme* (1921), n. 10—Part III (Documents), Document 3; Synod of Ssu-ch'uan, c. VIII, n. 3—*Coll. Lacensis,* VI, 618-620.

[13] Reference may be made to what has been said on this matter in Chapter VI.

ing to the specifications of this agreement and obtain the proper permissions for expenditures of an extraordinary nature.[14]

Although the *Normae* make no mention of the rector's duties toward the Superior General of the religious institute, yet such duties certainly exist. The annual report submitted to the board of Ordinaries of the region should be sent to the Superior General of the religious institute. This is not demanded by the *Normae,* but it is necessary for the welfare of the seminary, for the Superior General must be kept well informed as to the needs of the seminary if his aid is to be expected. Since it is the duty of the Superior General to supply the seminary with competent officials and professors, the rector must keep him informed on the fitness, learning and health of the seminary's official personnel.

The Superior General should be informed whenever a professor or official must be removed or supplied, and, in general should be consulted in all difficulties of a more serious nature.[15] This is most natural, since the seminary is entrusted to the religious or missionary institute itself, and the rector as the immediate superior of the seminary, rules, not in his own name, but in the name of the institute to which the seminary is committed. Since the seminary is in the care of the institute, it remains a primary obligation of the institute to see to its proper management and constant improvement. If therefore the Ordinaries of the region must be kept informed on conditions in the seminary, one cannot doubt that the Superior General of the institute has the right to the same information.

### Article 2. Exemption of the Seminary from the Jurisdiction of the Local Pastor

The regional seminary with its adjacent property is exempt from the jurisdiction of the local pastor; the par-

[14] Cf. v. g., "Conventio . . . inter Ordinarios Regionis Eccl. de Fukien et Ordinem Praedicatorum," n. 5—*Archivum S. C. P. F.*, Fu-chou, n. 3102/37 prot.

[15] *Directorium,* nos. 374-375.

ochial duties compatible with the nature of a pious institute belong to the rector of the seminary, who in regard to the confessions of the students shall observe the spirit of canon 518, § 2, of the Code of Canon Law.[16]

The exemption granted to the regional seminary in number 16 of the *Normae* does not differ greatly from that which is granted to all seminaries in canon 1368 of the Code. There is one difference, namely, that in regard to the confessions of the students canon 1368 calls attention to the provisions of canon 891, whereas number 16 of the *Normae* wishes canon 518, § 2, to be consulted in this matter. The exemption granted to the regional seminary is certainly real or local in the sense that all the buildings which in any way pertain to the seminary are exempted from the jurisdiction of the local pastor. Included therefore are the infirmary, the chapel, the houses of men religious and of women religious attached to the seminary, the houses of servants provided that these houses are on the seminary grounds,[17] and finally the seminary's summer villa, even though it be at a great distance from the seminary itself.[18]

Since therefore the seminary is exempt from the pastor's jurisdiction, the rector of the seminary takes the place of the pastor for those who are actually at the seminary,[19] and enjoys pastoral rights, except for matters of matrimony, over all who are there, whether they belong to the family of the seminary or elsewhere, including therefore the officials, professors, students, sisters religious, servants, guests and visitors.[20]

[16] *Normae* (1934), n. 16—*Sylloge*, n. 183.

[17] *Directorium*, n. 326; Onclin, "De Rectoribus Seminariorum," *Jus Pontificium*, XV (1935), 297; Beste, *Introductio*, p. 668.

[18] S. C. Sem. et Stud. Univ., 26 iul. 1934—apud Bouscaren, *The Canon Law Digest* (2 vols. with a supplement, Milwaukee: Bruce Publishing Co., Vol. I, 1934; Vol. II, 1943; Supplement, 1949), II, 425-426 (hereafter cited *Digest*).

[19] Can. 1368; *Normae* (1934), n. 16—*Sylloge*, n. 183.

[20] Cf. Vermeersch, "De exemptione seminariorum," *Jus Pontificium*, II (1922), 70; Onclin, "De Rectoribus Seminariorum," *Jus Pon-*

Since parochial duties exist as the rector's obligation, he must either personally or through his delegates fulfill the office of preaching, administer the sacraments, provide for the Communion of the sick, the Holy Viaticum and Extreme Unction, and see to the Christian burial of those who die at the seminary.[21] He has the power to dispense from the law of feasts and of fasts according to the provisions of canon 1245, and since he is the rector of the seminary church he has the power to bless sacred vestments.[22]

The *Normae* state that parochial rights and duties compatible with the nature of a pious institute are confided to the rector of the seminary. Matrimonial matters are therefore excluded,[23] and the rector cannot validly assist at marriages except upon delegation from the local Ordinary or the local pastor, and beyond the cases of urgent necessity in which the local Ordinary has given approval, the rector must not allow marriages to be celebrated in the seminary church at all.[24]

Regarding the hearing of confessions, the *Normae* give a slightly different rule than canon 891. According to canon 891 the rector of a seminary is not to hear the confessions of students who live at the seminary, unless in some particular case a student freely and for some grave and urgent reason asks that his confession be heard by the rector. In a regional seminary, however, the rector is to be guided by the spirit of canon 518, § 2. He is therefore allowed to hear the confessions of those who freely and of their own accord come to him, but he should not do this habitually except for a grave cause. The wording of canon 518, § 2, and especially of the *Normae*, which state that the rector should act "ad mentem canonis 518, § 2," indicate that the rector of a regional seminary subject to the Sacred Congregation

*tificium*, XVI (1936), 74-75; Beste, *Introductio*, p. 668; Coronata, *Institutiones*, II, n. 944; Brys, *Compendium*, II, n. 802.

[21] Canons 1368; 462; 1218; 1222.

[22] Canons 480, § 3; 1304, 3°.

[23] Can. 1368.

[24] Canons 1094; 1095; 1109, § 2.

for the Propagation of the Faith, has more freedom in this matter than the rector of a diocesan seminary. The reason is evident: in places of the missions it may well be that even in the regional seminary there is a lack of proper confessors for the students. To be noted also is the fact that the restrictions with which the Code and the *Normae* invest the use of the power to hear confessions have reference only to the confessions of the students, not of other people at the seminary.[25]

The rector has only the rights of a pastor over the sisters religious attached to the regional seminary. Hence he has no special powers in regard to the conferences and confessions of the sisters, and in these matters the particular provisions of the Code must be observed. With regard to funerals of men religious who die in the seminary, the special law of religious seems to prevail over the seminary legislation, since the latter refers to anyone in the seminary, the former however to a very determined class of persons.[26] The funerals of sisters religious should be considered as a matter that falls within the scope of the rector's power.[27]

### *Ordinary Power*

The office of rector of a seminary is an ecclesiastical office in the strict sense, for it is permanently established by law, is conferred according to the norms of law, and carries with it a participation in ecclesiastical power.[28] The power given to the office of rector by canon 1368 and to the office of rector of a regional seminary by number 16 of the *Normae*, namely,

[25] Canons 1368 and 891; *Normae* (1934), n. 16—*Sylloge*, n. 183; Coronata, *Institutiones*, II, n. 944, nota 8; *Directorium*, n. 358.

[26] Cf. can. 1221; Beste, *Introductio*, p. 592; Coronata, *Institutiones*, II, n. 944; Onclin, "De Rectoribus Seminariorum," *Jus Pontificium*, XVI (1936), 77.

[27] Canons 1222 and 1368 collated with canon 1230, § 5. Special cases on funerals of seminarians, servants, visitors, etc., are considered by Vermeersch in the *Jus Pontificium*, II (1922), 71, and by Onclin in the same periodical, XVI (1936), 76-77.

[28] Cf. can. 145, § 1; Onclin, "De Rectoribus Seminariorum," *Jus Pontificium*, XV (1935), 292.

to carry out the parochial duties, must therefore be considered as ordinary power.[29] This power may be delegated to others,[30] to the exclusion however of the power to hear confessions, since this power cannot be delegated by pastors either.[31]

The authors commonly hold that the rector of the seminary may use his faculties in favor of his habitual subjects when the latter are absent from the seminary.[32] Although the authors assign widely divergent reasons for this opinion, its adoption seems safe in practice, for those who are habitually associated with the work and the life of the seminary—the professors, the students, the servants, the sisters religious—continue in their status as subjects of the rector even when absent for a period of time. The faculties which a pastor may use in favor of his subjects absent from the parochial territory, the rector may then use on his habitual subjects when they are absent from the seminary. The question is not clear from the wording of the Code or of the *Normae,* but since the denial of such power is by no means evident either from the nature of the case or from the law itself, it seems reasonable to acknowledge this power as belonging to the rector of the seminary.[33]

Finally, since the exemption of the seminary as granted in canon 1368 is not restricted to diocesan seminaries, all seminaries legitimately erected, be they diocesan, interdiocesan or regional, enjoy this privilege. If one consider the

[29] Canons 197, § 1 and 873, § 1; Ciprotti, "An Superior Seminarii iurisdictionem ordinariam habeat ad confessiones alumnorum audiendas?" *Apollinaris* (Romae, 1928—), VIII (1935), 282-284 et 609-610.

[30] Can. 199, § 1.

[31] PCI, 16 oct. 1919—*AAS,* XI (1919), 477.

[32] Thus Beste, *Introductio,* p. 668; Coronata, *Institutiones,* II, n. 944; Brys, *Compendium,* II, n. 802; Vermeersch, "De exemptione seminariorum," *Jus Pontificium,* II (1922), 70-71; Onclin, "De Rectoribus Seminariorum," *Jus Pontificium,* XVI (1936), 74-76; and others.

[33] Cf. canons 201, § § 2, 3, and 881, § 2. See also Coronata, *Institutiones,* II, n. 944, p. 300, nota 6.

interdiocesan seminary as legitimately erected only if it is constituted by papal authority, then only papal interdiocesan seminaries would enjoy the exemption granted by canon 1368.[34] The writer prefers the doctrine that interdiocesan seminaries, if established by the authority of the Bishops of the several dioceses and tolerated by the Holy See, are also legitimately erected, and therefore looks upon such seminaries as exempt from the parochial jurisdiction. This doctrine appears applicable even though the seminary is administered by a religious or missionary institute, provided that its purpose is the training of the secular clergy.

### *Jurisdiction of the Local Ordinary*

When the Scheut Fathers agreed to erect a central seminary for their missions in 1921, they sent to the Sacred Congregation for the Propagation of the Faith the general statutes for the administration of the proposed seminary. These statutes, were not approved by the Sacred Congregation, but a new set of statutes was drawn up for the administration of regional seminaries in China, and these statutes were sent to the newly erected central seminary of Ta-t'ung. These statutes are the *Norme* of 1921. In the general statutes drawn up by the Scheut Fathers it is stated: "The seminary and its adjacent property will constitute a territory exempt both from the parochial jurisdiction and from the jurisdiction of the local Ordinary; the parochial rights and duties, as well as the rights, duties and privileges of the Ordinary will pertain to the rector."[35]

The Sacred Congregation did not accept this provision of the statutes. Exemption from the local pastor's jurisdiction was granted by the *Norme* of 1921, but exemption from episcopal jurisdiction was not granted. On the contrary it was stated: "Ordinary jurisdiction over the regional seminary is held by all the Ordinaries of the region, who shall

[34] Thus, v. g., Coronata, *Institutiones*, II, n. 944.

[35] "Projet d' Organisation et d' Administration du Séminaire Central de Tatung," n. 7—Part III (Documents), Document 2.

exercise it through the Ordinary of the place where the seminary is erected." And, "It is the exclusive right of the local Ordinary to be vigilant concerning the observance of the rules of the Institute, the scholastic program and the entire administration. He also has the right to put into execution the resolutions agreed upon in the annual meeting of the Ordinaries of the region."[36]

The *Normae* of 1934 drop these two provisions of the *Norme* of 1921. No mention is made of the jurisdiction of the Ordinaries of the region over the seminary, nor is the local Ordinary given the exclusive right of vigilance over the entire administration of the seminary. Nor is he granted power to put into execution the resolutions of the board of Ordinaries. Moreover, the rights of the Ordinaries are very much abbreviated by the *Normae* of 1934. They no longer have the power to draw up the rules of discipline, the scholastic program, the list of textbooks; they cannot appoint the professors and officials; they cannot present a candidate for the office of rector.

The entire administration of the seminary is entrusted to a religious or missionary institute, and the Ordinaries of the region are left the right to examine the annual report and to present their recommendations to the rector of the seminary. They are not given the power to enforce these recommendations. Therefore, although the *Normae* of 1934 do not grant a special exemption from the jurisdiction of the Ordinaries, yet one cannot but conclude that for all practical purposes the seminary enjoys an equivalent exemption in most matters of internal administration.

By reason of the element of territory, however, the regional seminary seems, at least in a limited way, subject to the jurisdiction of the local Ordinary. Although the seminary belongs to the Holy See, and it is proper that the local Ordinary have no more jurisdiction over the internal administration of the seminary than do the other Ordinaries of the region, yet the physical presence of the seminary and of its

[36] *Norme* (1921), nos. 5, 9—Part III (Documents), Document 3.

personnel within the territory of the diocese argues for the recognition of a limited jurisdiction of the local Ordinary over the seminary, since the seminary is not expressly exempted by the *Normae* or by the common law.

The special jurisdiction which the local Ordinary enjoys over the seminary seems to be that which may be regarded as necessary and essential for the common good of the diocese and the averting of harm from his territory. Consequently the local Ordinary possesses the right and the duty to urge upon the officials and students of the seminary the observance of the laws of the Church, and to guard the integrity of faith and morals. He must also guard against abuses in the administration of the sacraments and sacramentals, in the divine worship, in the veneration of the saints, and with regard to preaching and to indulgences. In order to fulfill these duties, but only with regard to the matters mentioned, he could visit the seminary canonically as well as coerce delinquents by means of appropriate penalties.[37]

The local Ordinary cannot however interfere in the administration of the seminary as such, since this administration has been committed to the religious or missionary institute, and the *Normae* give neither the Ordinaries of the region nor the local Ordinary any power to enforce the rules of discipline, the program of studies, the exercises of piety, or to appoint and remove officials and professors. The right and the duty to care for these matters of internal administration belong to the institute to which the seminary is committed,[38] immediately indeed to the rector of the seminary, who represents his institute in the seminary,[39] ultimately however to the Superior General of the institute, who may if he wishes hold a canonical visitation of the seminary regarding these matters.[40]

[37] Canons 335; 336; 344, § 1.
[38] *Normae* (1934), nos. 1, 3, 4, 7—*Sylloge*, n. 183.
[39] *Normae* (1934), n. 14—*Sylloge*, n. 183.
[40] *Directorium*, n. 318.

Since the regional seminary is an institution which belongs to the Holy See, and not to the mission in which it is located, and since the seminary is ruled by a religious or missionary institute in the name of and by the authority of the Holy See,[41] the *Normae* give to the local Ordinary no more jurisdiction over the seminary, considered precisely as a seminary, than that which is already enjoyed by the Ordinaries of the region collectively. These Ordinaries (and especially the local Ordinary in their name) have the right of vigilance over the administration of the seminary, and if they discover that the rules of discipline are not observed, that the decrees of the Holy See are not enforced, that the professors are incompetent, that the funds are not handled properly, etc., they most certainly must report such abuses to the Superior General of the religious institute and to the Sacred Congregation for the Propagation of the Faith whose duty it will be to take effective measures to correct them.

### ARTICLE 3. DIFFERENCES IN THE *Norme* OF 1921

The rights and duties of the rector of the regional seminary as outlined by the *Norme* of 1921 are not essentially different from those contained in the *Normae* of 1934. The rector is the immediate superior of the seminary and has the same control over the observance of the rules of discipline, over the exercises of piety, the program of studies and the financial administration. He must present a detailed spiritual and economic report to the board of Ordinaries each year, and must expedite the necessary documents before the ordinations of the students. He is given the additional duty of sending reports on the piety and the learning of the students to their respective Ordinaries several times a year, and is granted the additional right of voicing his preferences before the Ordinaries appoint professors, the spiritual director, the procurator and other officials of the seminary.[42]

[41] *Normae* (1934), n. 1—*Sylloge*, n. 183.

[42] *Norme* (1921), nos. 7, 10, 12—Part III (Documents), Document 3.

The seminary is declared exempt from the jurisdiction of the local pastor, and the parochial duties compatible with the nature of a pious institute are attributed to the rector of the seminary.[43]

These provisions of the *Norme* are very similar to those of the *Normae* of 1934. The *Norme* of 1921 however are very explicit in the matter of episcopal jurisdiction over the regional seminary, and give especially to the local Ordinary more power than do the regulations of 1934. The Ordinaries have the right to appoint and to dismiss the professors and the officials; they may present a candidate for the office of rector; they draw up the rules of discipline, the program of studies, the list of textbooks. All the Ordinaries retain ordinary jurisdiction over the seminary, which is however to be exercised by the Ordinary of the place where the seminary is erected.

The local Ordinary has the exclusive right of vigilance over the rules of discipline, the program of studies and the entire administration of the seminary, and is granted the right to put into execution the resolutions adopted by the board of Ordinaries at the annual meeting.[44] Consequently, contrary to the new *Normae* of 1934, the *Norme* of 1921 grant to the Ordinaries the right of active participation in the internal administration of the regional seminary, with the power to effect changes and to enforce their recommendations.

[43] *Norme* (1921), n. 11.
[44] *Norme* (1921), nos. 2, 3, 5, 7, 9.

# PART III

# DOCUMENTS

## Document 1

## Note Relative à un Séminaire Régional pour la Chine du Centre et du Nord.[1]

La question d'un séminaire régional pour la Chine du Sud comporte une solution rapide et simple que j'ai suggérée dans une note relative au Séminaire Général du Pulo Penang.

Mais pour le reste de la Chine, c'est plus compliqué. Il y a, à mon sens, 2 catégories des Missions qu'il n'est ni utile ni opportun d'obliger à envoyer leurs sujets à un Séminaire commun. Ce sont:

1° Les Missions qui, appartenant à une même Société Religieuse, veulent sérieusement fonder un Séminaire commun. Telles peut-être, les Missions Belges de Scheut et les Missions Italiennes du Honan.

2° Les Missions qui, grâce à leur activité, à leurs ressources, à leur dévelopement, ont mis leurs Séminaires sur un pied satisfaisant. On en trouve au Kiang Nan, au Tche Kiang, au Chantong, au Tchely, en Mongolie, au Sutchuen,[2] etc. etc.

Mais il existe une 3° catégorie de Missions nombreuses qui n'ont pas et n'auront pas avant très longtemps de Séminaire sérieux pour la Philosophie et la Théologie.

Il serait chimérique d'attendre que ces Missions, même pressées par Rome, s'entendent et s'organisent pour créer un Séminaire commun.

[1] *Archivum S. C. P. F.*, n. 2378/20 prot., rub. 130. This note gives the recommendations of Bishop Jean-Baptiste Budes de Guébriant, M.E.P., concerning a regional seminary for North China. It was made after the apostolic visitation of 1919-1920, and is dated 1 June, 1920.

[2] That is, Chiang-nan, Che-chiang, Shan-tung, Chih-li (Ho-pei), Mongolia, Ssu-ch'uan.

Le seul moyen, coûteux mais efficace, me parait être, l'établissement en Chine, dans une localité bien choisie et d'accès facile, auctoritate S. Pontificis, d'un Séminaire régional où toutes les Missions *pourraient* et où les Missions retardataires devraient envoyer leurs sujets.

Tchefou au Chantong septentrional[3] me paraîtrait pour maintes raisons (climat, communications, liberté à l'écart des Missions puissants, etc.) un point bien choisi.

Si l'on confie la direction à une de sociétés exerçant le ministère en Chine, je redoute qu'il n'y ait à craindre des jalousies et des plaintes.

C'est pourquoi je suggère la très digne et modeste Société de Saint Sulpice, uniquement vouée à la formation des clercs séculiers et qui a fait ses preuves hors d'Europe, en Amérique et au Canada. Elle a une branche française et une branche américaine. Elle est très généralement sympathique et ne porte ombrage à personne. J'imagine qu'elle consentirait même un concours matériel à l'Oeuvre. Et ce concours s'ajoutant à celui de plusieurs Missions, et à l'aide prêtée par la Sacrée Congrégation de la Propagande, permettrait sans doute d'aborder le problème d'une réalisation prochaine, même par son état financier.

L'objection qu'il faut des missionnaires de Chine pour former des prêtres chinois ne me semble avoir aucune valeur. Ce qu'il faut ce sont des prêtres dévoués et désintéressés, hors de tout soupçon d'ambition, pleins de l'esprit sacerdotal et apostolique.

✠ J. de Guébriant-Visiteur Apostolique pour la Chine.

## Document 2

### Projet d'Organisation et d'Administration du Séminaire Central de Tatung.[1]

1° Les Ordinaires des Missions de Scheut en Chine ont décidé l'érection à Tatung d'un séminaire central pour les

[3] Chih-fou (Chefoo) in North Shan-tung.

[1] *Archivum S. C. P. F.*, n. 1025/21 prot., rub. 130.

élèves de leurs missions respectives se préparant au sacerdoce; ils consentent à ce que des élèves d'autres missions y soient admis, si le Recteur de l'établissement juge que les circonstances le permettent.

2° Les mêmes Ordinaires pourvoiront aux frais d'installation et d'administration générale du séminaire, dans la mesure et aussi longtemps que le séminaire sera incapable d'y pourvoir de ses propres fonds. A cette fin chacun des Vicariats Ap. de Mongolie et du Kansu feront un versement initial de 2,000 taels (soit chacun environ 20,000 frs). Quant aux frais d'entretien des élèves, ils seront couverts par des pensions annuelles payées par les Ordinaires respectifs.

3° Les mêmes Ordinaires expriment le désir que, vu la pénurie des ressources de leurs missions, il puisse être obtenu d'ailleurs des fonds qui permettraient au séminaire de pourvoir par lui-même aux frais de son administration générale. En particulier ils jugent que l'acqusition ou la construction d'un séminaire définitif constituerait une charge au dessus de leurs forces.

4° Le Séminaire une fois constitué relévera directement de l'autorité de la S. C. de la Propagande et constituera la propriété de la même S. C. avec tous ses biens mobiliers et immobiliers.

5° Le Recteur du séminaire sera nommé par le Cardinal Préfet de la Propagande sur la présentation des Ordinaires et du Supérieur Général de Scheut.

6° Pour le personnel attaché au séminaire, le Recteur dans chaque cas proposera deux ou plusieurs candidats à chacun des Ordinaires: il transmettra au Supérieur Général de Scheut les appréciations et propositions qu'il en aura obtenues en y joignant les siennes propres: il appartiendra au même Supérieur Général de choisir parmi les candidats proposés et le choix ainsi fait sera exécuté d'office. Le collège des Ordinaires ainsi que le Supérieur Général de Scheut et même le Recteur du séminaire avec l'assentiment des deux Ordinaires, dont il est parlé au 9°, peuvent, pour motif grave, retirer ou éloigner du séminaire quelqu'un du personnel.

7° Le séminaire avec ses dépendances et jardins adjacents constituera un territoire exempt tant de la jurisdiction paroissiale que de celle de l'Ordinaire du lieu : les droits et les devoirs paroissiaux, ainsi que les droits, devoirs et privilèges de l'Ordinaire seront dévolus au Recteur.

8° C'est au collège des Ordinaires qu'il appartient de régler *jure communi* ce qui regarde l'administration du séminaire dans les choses qui touchent à la discipline, à l'enseignement et aux finances, comme aussi de veiller à l'exécution de ce qui aura été statué. A cette fin le collège des Ordinaires se réunira en temps opportun et le Recteur du séminaire sera appel d'office à ces réunions. Le collège des Ordinaires peut déléguer quelqu'un de ses membres pour faire la visite du séminaire.

9° Il sera constitué à l'intérieur du séminaire un conseil de discipline. Pour les choses de plus grande importance que le Recteur ne peut ou ne veut décider par lui-même, il prendra conseil auprès de deux membres du collège des Ordinaires, que ceux-ci auront délégués à cet effet, et décidera avec eux.

10° Pour ce qui regarde le règlement intérieur du séminaire, on se conformera, pour autant que les conditions du pays le permettent, au règlement disciplinaire prescrit par la S. C. des Evêques et Réguliers, le 18 Janvier 1908, pour les séminaires d'Italie. En particulier le séminaire sera et restera une institution séparée de toute autre institution d'enseignement, et une clôture assez sévère y sera maintenue pour que l'esprit du monde n'y puisse pas pénétrer.

## Document 3

## Norme per i Seminari Regionali in Cina[1]

### I. Alta Direzione

1. Il Seminario Regionale è posto sotto l'alta direzione della Sacra Congregazione di Propaganda Fide.

[1] Datae a S. C. de Prop. Fide, die 14 mart. 1921—*Archivum S. C. P. F.*, n. 3436/21 prot., rub. 8.

2. Gli Ordinari della Regione, di commune accordo, sottoporranno all' approvazione della S. Congregazione di Propaganda Fide:

a) la scelta, da loro fatta, del luogo dove deve sorgere il Seminario regionale.

b) il regolamento disciplinare del Seminario.

c) il programma degli studi, la distribuzione delle materie e delle ore di insegnamento nei singoli corsi ed i libri di testo.

d) il bilancio preventivo sia degli introiti del Seminario, con l'indicazione della proporzione del contributo delle varie missioni, sia delle spese occorrenti per il funzionamento dell'Istituto.

3. a) La nomina del Rettore spetta alla Sacra Congregazione di Propaganda su proposta degli Ordinari.

b) La nomina dei Professori sarà sottoposta alla conferma della Propaganda, come pure il loro licenziamento sarà almeno notificato alla Sacra Congregazione per essere ratificato.

4. Al Seminario dovranno mandarsi tutti gli alunni di Filosofia e di Teologia della regione; e gli Ordinari non potranno ritirare dal medesimo i propri alunni, per educarli altrove, senza l'autorizzazione della S. Congregazione di Propaganda.

II. Attribuzioni degli Ordinari della Regione

5. La Giurisdizione ordinaria sul Seminario regionale appartiene a tutti gli Ordinari della regione, i quali la eserciteranno per mezzo dell'Ordinario del luogo.

6. a) Essi ogni anno si aduneranno per trattare delle cose riguardanti sia la disciplina, sia gli studi, sia l'amministrazione temporale dell'Istituto; e a questo fine esamineranno la relazione scritta che su ciò presenterà il Rettore del Seminario.

b) Al convegno annuale degli Ordinari presiederà il Vescovo del luogo, o, in sua assenza, il piu anziano; fungerà da Segretario un altro Ordinario, il più giovane di nomina.

7. Agli Ordinari di comune accordo spetterà di nominare o di licenziare il Padre spirituale, l'economo, gli altri superiori e gli insegnanti del Seminario, sentito il parere del Rettore del Seminario.

8. Gli Ordinari potranno, finiti tutti gli studi, ordinare i loro alunni nella propria missione, ovvero concedere le lettere dimissorie perchè siano ordinati dall' Ordinario del luogo dove sorge il Seminario.

## III. Attribuzioni dell' Ordinario del Luogo

9. Spetta esclusivamente all' Ordinario del luogo il vigilare sull' osservanza del regolamento, dei programmi scolastici e su tutto l'andamento del Seminario, come pure il mandare in esecuzione le disposizioni prese d' accordo, nell' adunanza annuale, dagli Ordinari della regione.

## IV. Del Rettore

10. Egli è il Superiore del Seminario, da lui dipenderà direttamente tutto il personale insegnante e dirigente, a lui quindi l'Ordinario del luogo avrà cura di comunicare le disposizioni relative al funzionamento dell' Istituto, ed egli stesso procurerà di essere in frequente relazione coll' Ordinario del luogo. Ogni anno presenterà all' adunanza dei Vescovi la relazione morale ed economica dell' Istituto, come si è detto all' art. 5; e periodicamente, durante l'anno, invierà ai singoli Ordinari un'esatta relazione sulla condotta e sul profitto dei rispettivi alunni.

11. Il Seminario, con le sue adiacenze, è immune dalla giurisdizione del quasi-parroco; gli offici parrocchiali, consentanei alla natura del pio Istituto, sono attribuiti al Rettore del Seminario, il quale però li eserciterà per mezzo del direttore spirituale.

12. Prima delle S. Ordinazioni sarà cura del Rettore provvedere alla spedizione e raccolta dei documenti necessari; però, dopo averne preso nota, li trasmetterà agli Ordinari, procurando di informarsi per tempo delle loro intenzioni circa il luogo dove avverrà l'ordinazione dei singoli alunni.

## Document 4

## Conventio Ordinariorum pro Seminario Regionali de Hongkong[1]

Hong-Kong, die 22 februarii 1927. Infrascripti Vicarii Apostolici, ad cleri institutionem quo meliori potest modo prospicientes, haec quae sequuntur, statuunt:

1. Quas Summus Pontifex Pius XI in Encyclica RERUM ECCLESIAE normas et praecepta de re missionaria impartit, toto corde amplectentes observantesque, de condendo Seminario Regionali in Hongkong libenti animo conveniunt.

2. RR. Patribus e Societate Iesu Seminarium concreditur regendum normis quas S. C. de Propaganda Fide erit datura.

3. Quos Vicarii Apostolici singuli mittunt alumnos sumptu cuiusque suo alendos, Patres e Societate Iesu gratuite ad normas iuris instituunt. Linguam anglicam seu gallicam alumni discent, iuxta Vicariorum Apostolicorum instructiones.

4. Vicarii Apostolici grates Pontificio Operi Sancti Petri pro munifica caritate ex corde agunt, conditione admissa solvendi per 20 annos foenus 2½% super aere aedificandae domo supellectilibusque instruendae expendendo.

5. Seminarii Regionalis proprietas ad S. C. de Propaganda Fide, usus vero ad Vicarios Apostolicos pertinet, ratione habita eorum participationis in constituendo seminario inque solvendis foeneribus per 20 annos. Repraesentatio legalis coram gubernio ad Vicarium Apostolicum de Hongkong deputatur vel, ex eiusdem delegatione, ad Seminarii Rectorem. Nulla vero radicalis mutatio vel bonorum alienatio fiet inconsulta Sacra Congregatione de Propaganda Fide.

6. Missionibus in meridionalibus Sinarum partibus erigendis, sive sinensibus sive exteris, integrum erit, sub allatis normis, in partem Seminarii Regionalis accedere.

[1] This document is attached as an appendix to a report of the Apostolic Delegate in China, dated 28 Febr., 1927—*Archivum S. C. P. F.*, Hsiang-kang (Hongkong), n. 1299/27 prot.

7. Domus concreditur RR. Patribus Societatis Iesu, Seminariique Rector curam habebit omnia servandi.

✠ Antonius Fourquet—Vicarius Apostolicus de Canton.
✠ Henricus Valtorta—Vicarius Apostolicus de Hongkong
✠ A. Gautier—Vicarius Apostolicus de Pakhoi
✠ José da Costa Nunes—Episcopus Macaon [ensis]
Sac. Joannes Guarona—Vicarius Delegatus Shiuchow
Jacobus Walsh—Praefectus Apostolicus de Kongmoon, *et pro futuris missionibus de Maryknoll in Swatow et Kwangsi.*

## Document 5

Conventio circa administrativam gestionem Seminarii Regionalis de Fukien in Foochow erecti inter RR. mos DD. Ordinarios Regionis eccl. de Fukien et S. Ordinem Praedicatorum[1]

1. Seminarium Regionale de Fukien in civitate Foochow erectum est Seminarium Maius ad alumnos ex tota Regione ecclesiastica de Fukien ad sacerdotium adspirantes educandos efformandosque. Proprietas huius Seminarii ad S. Sedem pertinet, quae eius gubernium S. Ordini Praedicatorum commisit; usus vero eiusdem Seminarii ad Rev. mos Ordinarios Regionis de Fukien pertinet, qui regulariter omnes suos alumnos Philosophiae et Theologiae ad illud mittere tenentur.

Repraesentatio legalis huius Seminarii coram gubernio civili ad Vicarium Apostolicum de Foochow deputatur, qui etiam Relator est inter Ordinarios Regionis et Rectorem Seminarii.

2. Seminarii Regionalis regimen universum et administratio regitur Normis a S. Congregatione de Propaganda Fide statutis (can. 1357 § 4) scilicet "Normis pro Seminariis Regionalibus commissis Institutis Religiosis vel Missionalibus a S. Congregatione de Propaganda Fide approbatis per Rescriptum diei 27. Aprilis 1934, No. 1989/34 cum Allegato."

[1] Archivum S. C. P. F., Fu-chou (Foochow), n. 3102/37 prot.

3. Onus pecunia sustentandi Seminarium Regionale incumbit Rev. mis Ordinariis Regionis, Ordini Praedicatorum autem onus administrandi. Hinc Ordo Praedicatorum nullam contrahit obligationem quoad debita forte contracta vel contrahenda in futuro a Seminario; sed Rector Seminarii nulla debita contrahere potest absque licentia Ordinariorum.

4. Expensae ordinariae tam alumnorum quam moderatorum et professorum Seminarii ab Ordinariis Regionis pecunia solvuntur pro rata parte alumnorum cuiusque divisionis ecclesiasticae in Seminario degentium.

5. Rector Seminarii nullas incurrat expensas extraordinarias sine licentia praevia in scriptis obtenta vel a consilio Ordinariorum, vel in casu urgenti saltem ab Ordinario loci.

In rebus autem disciplinae Seminarii, e.gr. si agitur de aliquo alumno admittendo vel dimittendo, Rector ipse decidet, collato tamen consillio [sic], si casus fert, cum aliis moderatoribus.

6. Si quando de regimine Seminarii in re quacumque dissentitur inter Consilium Ordinariorum et S. Ordinem Praedicatorum, causa ad S. Congregationem de Propaganda Fide decernenda deferatur.

7. Conventio haec nonnisi de mutuo consensu Consilii Ordinariorum et S. Ordinis Praedicatorum nec rescindi nec essentialiter mutari potest, sine mensium duodecim noticia et S. Congregationis de Propaganda Fide approbatione.

## CONCLUSIONS

As a result of this work the following conclusions are offered:

1. Although the Code of Canon Law states that the entire management and administration of an interdiocesan or regional seminary is governed by rules established by the Holy See (can. 1357, § 4), such seminaries as were erected by episcopal authority before the promulgation of the Code may be allowed to exist and to function without subjection to special norms of the Holy See. (pp. 63-68).

2. Since the Holy See has not insisted on a strict interpretation of the final clause of canon 1354, § 3, and the fourth paragraph of canon 1357, interdiocesan seminaries erected by the Bishops without the permission of the Holy See may be tolerated, even though such seminaries were erected after the promulgation of the Code of Canon Law. (pp. 62-68).

3. The *praxis* of the Sacred Congregation for the Propagation of the Faith has introduced a juridical distinction between the regional seminary and the interdiocesan seminary. The regional seminary is a seminary common to several dioceses, erected by the Holy See, and governed by special norms established by the Holy See; the interdiocesan seminary is a seminary common to several dioceses, but which has been erected by the authority of the Bishops concerned, and is not governed by the special norms of the Holy See. (pp. 68-70).

4. When a seminary is constituted a regional seminary according to the provisions of the *Normae* of 1934, the property rights over the seminary's movable and immovable goods are thereby vested in the Holy See, at least by a virtual and implicit contract of donation. (pp. 77-79).

5. Ordinaries are obliged to send their students to a regional seminary only if the seminary has been erected also for the service of their dioceses, regardless of the geographic location of the dioceses and the seminary. (pp. 80-83).

6. Those students of regional seminaries in China who are ordained to major orders *titulo missionis* are excluded from entrance into a religious institute by the final provision of canon 542, 1°, of the Code of Canon Law. (pp. 84-89).

7. Since the regional seminary is proper to all the dioceses it serves according to its decree of erection, seminarians who study in a regional seminary for one of these dioceses acquire a domicile in the particular diocese for which they are studying. Hence a Bishop who has students 21 years of age in a regional seminary may consider these students as having a domicile in his diocese and may promote them to first tonsure for the service of his diocese or mission, even though the students have never actually been physically present in the diocese, vicariate, or prefecture itself. (pp. 118-119).

8. Although the *Normae* of 1934 do not grant an express exemption from the jurisdiction of the Ordinaries of the region, yet for all practical purposes the regional seminary that is subject to the Sacred Congregation for the Propagation of the Faith and is entrusted to a religious or missionary institute enjoys an equivalent exemption in most matters of internal administration; a notable exception to this rule are the rights over the economic administration granted to the Ordinaries by the agreement entered into with the Superior General of the institute to which the seminary is entrusted. (pp. 130-131).

9. By reason of the element of territory, the regional seminary is in a limited way subject to the jurisdiction of the local Ordinary. It is his right and duty to urge the observance of the laws of the Church, to preserve the integrity of faith and morals, and to safeguard ecclesiastical discipline against abuse. He cannot however interfere with the internal administration of the seminary. (pp. 143-146).

## BIBLIOGRAPHY

### Sources

*Acta Apostolicae Sedis, Commentarium Officiale,* Romae, 1909—

*Acta et Decreta Sacrorum Conciliorum Recentiorum, Collectio Lacensis,* 7 vols., Freiburgi Brisgoviae: Herder, 1870-1892.

*Acta Ecclesiae Mediolanensis,* 4 vols., Milan, 1890-1892.

*Acta Sanctae Sedis,* 41 vols., Romae, 1865-1908.

Bouscaren, T. Lincoln, *The Canon Law Digest,* 2 vols. with a supplement, Milwaukee: Bruce, 1934, 1943, 1949.

*Bullarum Diplomatum et Privilegiorum Sanctorum Romanorum Pontificum Taurinensis editio,* 25 vols., Augustae Taurinorum, 1857-1872.

*Codex Iuris Canonici Pii X Pontificis Maximi iussu digestus, Benedicti Papae XV auctoritate promulgatus,* Romae: Typis Polyglottis Vaticanis, 1917.

*Codicis Iuris Canonici Fontes cura Emi Petri Card. Gasparri editi,* 9 vols., Romae (postea Civitate Vaticana): Typis Polyglottis Vaticanis, 1923-1939 (Vols. VII-IX ed. *cura et studio Emi Iustiniani Card. Serédi*).

*Collectanea Commissionis Synodalis,* Peiping: Commissio Synodalis in Sinis, 1928-1947; *China Missionary,* Shanghai, 1948—

*Collectanea Constitutionum, Decretorum, Indultorum ac Instructionum Sanctae Sedis ad Usum Operariorum Apostolicorum Societatis Missionum ad Exteros,* Parisiis: Typis Georges Chamerot, 1880.

*Collectanea S. Congregationis de Propaganda Fide,* 2 vols., Romae: Typographia Polyglotta, S. C. de Propaganda Fide, 1907.

*Concilii Tridentini, Diariorum, Actorum, Epistolarum, Tractatuum, Nova Collectio.* Edidit Societas Goerresiana, 13 vols., Freiburgi Brisgoviae: Herder, 1901—

*Enchiridion Clericorum, Documenta Ecclesiae Sacrorum Alumnis Instituendis,* Romae: Typis Polyglottis Vaticanis, 1938.

Hardouin, Jean, *Acta Conciliorum et Epistolae Decretales ac Constitutiones Summorum Pontificum,* 12 vols., Parisiis, 1714-1715.

*Ius Pontificium de Propaganda Fide,* ed. R. de Martinis, *Pars Prima,* 7 vols. in 8 (Vol. VIII, Supplementum et Index), Romae, 1888-1897; *Pars Secunda,* 1 vol., Romae, 1909.

Mansi, Ioannes, *Sacrorum Conciliorum Nova et Amplissima Collectio,* 53 vols. in 60, Parisiis, 1901-1927.

*Primum Concilium Sinense—Acta—Decreta et Normae—Vota, etc.,* Zi-ka-wei: Typographia Missionis Catholicae, 1929.

Schroeder, H., *Canons and Decrees of the Council of Trent,* St. Louis: Herder, 1941.

*Statuta pro Missionibus Ordinis Fratrum Minorum*, Ad Claras Aquas: Typographia Collegii S. Bonaventurae, 1950.

*Sylloge Praecipuorum Documentorum Recentium Summorum Pontificum et S. Congregationis de Propaganda Fide Necnon Aliarum SS. Congregationum Romanarum ad usum Missionariorum*, Romae: Typis Polyglottis Vaticanis, 1939.

### Unpublished Sources

Archivum Sacrae Congregationis de Propaganda Fide:
Chi-lin (Kirin), 1935-1940.
Chi-nan (Tsinan), 1934-1936.
Ching-hsien (Kinghsien), 1941.
Fu-chou (Foochow), 1936-1937.
Han-k'ou (Hankow), 1931-1933.
Hsiang-kang (Hongkong), 1926-1950.
K'ai-feng, 1931-1932.
Lan-chou (Lanchow), 1938.
Mongolia Orientalis, 1921.
Pei-p'ing (Peiping), 1934.
Shang-hai, 1947.
Sinae—Negotia Communia (Cina—Affari Comuni), 1919-1934.
Süan-hua (Süanhwa), 1932.
Sui-yüan, 1936-1941.
T'ai-yüan, 1934-1936.
Ta-t'ung, 1930-1935.
Wu-hu. 1947.

### Reference Works

Berutti, C., *Institutiones Iuris Canonici*, 6 vols. in 7, Vol. IV, 1940, Taurini-Romae: Marietti.

Beste, Udalricus, *Introductio in Codicem*, 2 ed., Collegeville, Minn.: St. John's Abbey Press, 1944.

Bouscaren, T. Lincoln-Ellis, Adam C., *Canon Law, Text and Commentary*, Milwaukee: Bruce Publishing Co., 1946.

Brys, J., *Juris Canonici Compendium*, 10 ed., 2 vols., olim ab Exc. mo De Brabandere et R. dis Adm. Van Coillie et De Meester editum, Brugis: Desclée, 1947-1949.

Cappello, Felix, *Summa Iuris Canonici*, 3 vols., Romae: apud Aedes Universitatis Gregorianae, 1940-1945. Vols. I et II, 4. ed., 1945; Vol. III, 2. ed., 1940.

Coronata, Matthaeus Conte a, *Institutiones Iuris Canonici ad Usum Utriusque Cleri et Scholarum*, 2. ed., 5 vols., Romae: Marietti, 1939-1947.

———,*Institutiones Iuris Canonici ad Usum Utriusque Cleri et*

*Scholarum, de Sacramentis, Tractatus Canonicus,* 3 vols., Romae: Marietti, 1943-1946.

Cracco, A., *De Seminariorum Sinensium Institutione,* Shanghai: Don Bosco Industrial School Press, 1946.

*Directorium Seminariorum in Sinis,* Pekini: Auctoribus de Scheut, 1949.

Ferraris, Lucius, *Prompta Bibliotheca Canonica, Iuridica Moralis, Theologica, necnon Ascetica, Polemica, Rubricistica, Historica,* 9 vols., Romae, 1885-1899.

Genicot, E.-Salsmans, J., *Institutiones Theologiae Moralis,* 16 ed., 2 vols., Bruxellis, 1946.

Grentrup, Theodorus, *Ius Missionarium,* Steyl, Holland: Typographia domus Missionum a S. Michaele Arch., 1925.

Gubbels, Natalis, *Praxis Missionalis in Vicariatu Apostolico de Ichang,* Wuchang: The Franciscan Press, 1935.

Hinschius, Paulus, *System des katholischen Kirchenrechts,* 4 vols., Berlin: Guttentag, 1869-1888.

Langasco, A., *De Institutione Clericorum in Disciplinis Inferioribus,* Romae: Typis Polyglottis Vaticanis, 1936.

Leyssen, J., *Formatio Cleri in Mongolia,* Pekini: Impr. des Lazaristes, 1940.

Masarei, Seraphino, *De Missionum Institutione ac de Relationibus inter Superiores Missionum et Superiores Religiosos,* Romae: apud Institutum Graphicum Tiberinum, 1940.

Micheletti, *Ius Pianum,* Augustae Taurinorum: Marietti, 1914.

Orsenigo, C., *Life of St. Charles Borromeo,* St. Louis: Herder, 1945.

Pallavicino, S., *Istoria del Concilio di Trento,* 3 vols., Naples, 1757.

Paventi, Xaverius, *De Iuramento ac de Titulo Missionis,* Romae: Officium Libri Catholici, 1946.

Schaefer, Timotheus, *De Religiosis,* 4. ed., Roma: Typis Polyglottis Vaticanis, 1947.

Vermeersch, A.-Creusen, J., *Epitome Iuris Canonici,* 6. ed., 3 vols., Mechliniae et Romae: H. Dessain, 1937-1946.

Vromant, G., *Ius Missionariorum de Personis,* Louvain: Museum Lessianum, 1935.

———, *Ius Missionariorum, Introductio et Normae Generales,* Louvain: Museum Lessianum, 1934.

Wernz, F.-Vidal, P., *Ius Canonicum,* 7 vols. in 9, Romae: Universitas Gregoriana, 1927-1946. Vol. II, 3. ed., 1943; Vol. V, 3. ed., 1946.

Woywod, Stanislaus, *A Practical Commentary on the Code of Canon Law,* 2 vols., 9th printing, revised by Callistus Smith, New York: Joseph F. Wagner, 1945.

Ybanez, C., *Directorium Missionariorum,* 2. ed., Barcinonae: apud Josephum Vilamala, 1921.

### Articles

Ciprotti, P., "An Superior Seminarii iurisdictionem ordinariam habeat ad confessiones alumnorum audiendas?" *Apollinaris,* VIII (1935), 282-284, 609-610.

Larraona, A., "Commentarium Codicis—Can. 542, 1° (cont.) et 2°," *Commentarium pro Religiosis et Missionariis,* XVII (1936), 236-246.

Onclin, W., "De Rectoribus Seminariorum," *Jus Pontificium,* XV (1935), 287-297; et XVI (1936), 69-77.

Vermeersch, A., "De exemptione seminariorum," *Jus Pontificium,* II (1922), 67-71.

### Periodicals

*Annuaire de l'Observatoire de Zi-ka-wei,* Shanghai, 1901-1922; *Missions, séminaires, écoles en Chine,* 1923-1932; *Annuaire des Missions Catholiques de Chine,* 1933-1947; *Annuaire de l'Eglise Catholique en Chine,* 1948—

*Apollinaris,* Romae, 1928—

*Apostolicum—Periodicum Pastorale et Asceticum pro Missionibus,* Tsinanfu, 1930—

*Commentarium pro Religiosis,* Romae, 1920; ab anno 1935: *Commentarium pro Religiosis et Missionariis.*

*Jus Pontificium,* Romae, 1921-1940.

*Les Missions de Chine,* Shanghai, 1916-1942.

## ABBREVIATIONS

*AAS*—*Acta Apostolicae Sedis.*

*Acta Eccl. Med.*—*Acta Ecclesiae Mediolanensis.*

*Annuaire*—*Annuaire des Missions Catholique de Chine.*

*ASS*—*Acta Sanctae Sedis.*

*Bull. Rom.*—*Bullarum Diplomatum et Privilegiorum Sanctorum Romanorum Pontificum Taurinensis editio.*

*Coll. Comm. Syn.*—*Collectanea Commissionis Synodalis.*

*Coll. S. C. P. F.*—*Collectanea S. C. de Prop. Fide* ed. 1907.

Const.—constitutio.

Decr.—decretum.

Ep. encycl.—epistola encyclica.

*Fontes*—*Codicis Iuris Canonici Fontes cura ... Gasparri editi.*

Instr.—instructio.

*Ius Pont.*—*Ius Pontificium de Propaganda Fide.*

Litt. ap.—littera apostolica.

PCI—Pontificia Commissio ad Codicis Canones authentice Interpretandos.

*PCS*—*Primum Concilium Sinense—Acta—Decreta et Normae—Vota, etc.*

Prot.—numerus protocolli in archivo S. C. de Prop. Fide.

Rub.—numerus rubricae in archivo S. C. de Prop. Fide.

S. C. de Prop. Fide, aut, S. C. P. F.—Sacra Congregatio de Propaganda Fide.

S. C. Ep. et Reg.—Sacra Congregatio Episcoporum et Regularium.

S. C. Sem. et Stud. Univ.—Sacra Congregatio de Seminariis et Studiorum Universitatibus.

*Sylloge*—*Sylloge Praecipuorum Documentorum ... ad usum Missionariorum.*

# INDEX OF PLACE NAMES

I. Wade-Giles Transliteration

(Abbreviations: alt. n.—alternate name; mod. n.—modern name.)


An-ching (Anking), 51
An-hui (Anhwei), 51, 52
An-kuo (Ankwo), 43, 44

Ch'ang-te (Changteh), 53
Cha-la (Chala), Regional Seminary of, 43-44
Chao-hsien (Chaohsien), 43, 44
Che-chiang (Chekiang), 26, 27, 59, 69, 148
Cheng-ting (Chengting), 43, 44
Ch'eng-tu (Chengtu), 60
  Intermissional Seminary of, 60, 69
Chia-hsing (Kashing), 60
Chiang-chou (Kiangchow; mod. n. Hsin-chiang), 49
Chiang-hsi (Kiangsi), 27
Chiang-men (Kongmoon), 55, 57
Chiang-nan (Kiangnan), 26, 148
Chiang-su (Kiangsu), 45, 50, 51, 82
Chia-ting (Kiating), 60
Chien-ou (Kienow), 55
Chih-fou (Chefoo; mod. n. Yen-t'ai), 26, 29, 45, 46
Chih-li (Chihli; mod. n. Ho-pei), 26, 148
Chi-lin (Kirin), 41, 42
Chi-nan (Tsinan), 45, 46
  Regional Seminary of, 45-46, 69, 81
Ch'in-chou (Tsinchow), 49
Ching-chou (Kingchow; mod. n. Chiang-ling), 53
Ch'ing-hai (Tsinghai; Mongol: Kokonor), 50
Ching-hsien (Kinghsien), 44, 45, 81
  Regional Seminary of, 44-45, 51, 81, 82, 83
Ch'ing-tao (Tsingtao), 59
Chi-ning (Tsining), 39, 40, 48
Chou-chih (Chowchih), 49
Chou-ts'un (Chowtsun), 45, 46
Ch'ung-ch'ing (Chungking), 11, 60
  Major Seminary of, 60

Feng-hsiang (Fengsiang), 49
Fen-yang (Fenyang), 43, 82
Fu-chien (Fukien), 28, 54, 56, 79, 81, 155
  Regional Seminary of, 54-55, 56, 79, 81, 155-156
Fu-chou (Foochow; mod. n. Min-hou), 55
Fu-ning (Funing), 55

Hai-men (Haimen), 51
Han-chung (Hanchung; mod. n. Nan-cheng), 52
Hang-chou (Hangchow; mod. n. Hang-hsien), 60
Han-k'ou (Hankow), 53, 122
  Regional Seminary of, 52-54, 81, 122
Ho-nan (Honan), 26, 28, 52, 59
Ho-pei (Hopeh), 43, 45, 81, 82
Hsia-men (Amoy), 28, 55
Hsi-an (Sian; mod. n. Hsi-ching), 49
Hsiang-kang (Hongkong), 28, 55, 56
  Regional Seminary of 29, 55-58, 79, 154-155
Hsiang-kang-tzu (English: Aberdeen), 55

Hsien-hsien (Sienhsien), 44, 45, 81
Hsin-chiang (Sinkiang), 50
Hsin-ching (Hsinking; alt. n. Ch'ang-ch'un), 41, 42
Regional Seminary of, 41-42
Hsing-an (Hingan; mod. n. An-k'ang), 52
Hsin-hsiang (Sinsiang), 52, 59
Hsin-yang (Sinyang), 52, 59
Hsi-wan-tzu (Siwantze), 39, 40, 46, 48
Hsü-chia-hui (Zi-ka-wei), 18, 50, 51
Hsü-chou (Süchow; mod. n. T'ung-shan), 45, 51, 82, 83
Hu-nan (Hunan), 52, 53, 54, 81, 122
Hung-chia-lou (Hungkialou), 45
Hung-tung (Hungtung), 43, 82
Hu-pei (Hupeh), 27, 52, 53, 54, 81, 122

I-chou (Ichow; mod. n. Lin-i), 59
I-hsien (Yihsien), 43
I-tu-hsien (Iduhsien), 45, 46

Je-ho (Jehol), 39, 40, 42, 48

K'ai-feng (Kaifeng), Regional Seminary of, 52
K'ang-ting (Kangting; alt. n. Ta-chien-lu), 60
Kan-su (Kansu), 49, 50
Kuang-chou (Canton), 25, 55
Kuang-hsi (Kwangsi), 58
Kuang-tung (Kwangtung, 55, 56, 58
Kuei-chou (Kweichow), 11
Kuei-lin (Kweilin), 58
Kuei-sui (Kweisui; alt. n. Hou-ho), 48 in note 46
K'un-ming (Kunming), Major Seminary of, 60

Lan-chou (Lanchow; mod. n. Kao-lan), Regional Seminary of, 49-50
Li-chou (Lichow; mod. n. Li-hsien), 53
Lin-ch'ing (Lintsing), 45, 46
Li-shui (Lishui), 60
Lu-an (Luan; mod. n. Ch'ang-chih), 48, 49

Manchoukuo, 41, 42

Nan-ching (Nanking), 51, 52
Ning-hsia (Ningsia), 39, 40, 48
Ning-po (Ningpo; mod. n. Yin-hsien), 59, 60
Intermissional Seminary of, 59-60, 69
Ning-yüan (Ningyüan; mod. n. Hsi-ch'ang), 60

Pai-lu-ch'ang (Pehluchang), 60
Pang-fou (Pengpu), 51
Pao-ting (Paoting; mod. n. Ch'ing-yüan), 43, 44
Pei-ching (Peking; mod. n. Pei-p'ing), 43, 44
Pei-hai (Pakhoi), 55, 58

San-yüan (Sanyüan), 49
Shang-hai (Shanghai), 18, 50, 51
Regional Seminary of, 50-51, 59, 82
Shan-hsi (Shansi), 40, 43, 48, 49, 82
Shan-t'ou (Swatow), 58
Shan-tung (Shantung), 26, 29, 45, 46, 52, 59, 69, 81, 148
Shao-chou (Shiuchow; mod. n. Ch'ü-chiang), 55
Shao-wu (Shaowu), 55
Shen-hsi (Shensi), 49, 52
Shun-ch'ing (Shunking; mod. n. Nan-ch'ung), 60
Shun-te (Shunteh; mod. n. Hsing-t'ai), 43, 44
Shuo-chou (Shohchow; mod. n. Shuo-hsien), 48, 49

Ssu-ch'uan (Szechwan), 11, 26, 60, 69, 148
Synod of, 11-13, 14, 17, 100
Süan-ch'eng (Süancheng), 51
Süan-hua (Süanhwa), 43
Regional Seminary of, 42-43, 82
Sui-fu (Suifu; mod. n. I-pin), 60
Sui-yüan (Suiyüan), 39, 40, 48
Regional Seminary of, 39-40, 42, 48, 59

Tai-chia-chuang (Taikiachuang), 59
T'ai-chou (Taichow; mod. n. Lin-hai), 60
T'ai-yüan (Taiyüan; mod. n. Yang-ch'ü), 48, 49
Regional Seminary of, 48-49, 82
Ta-ming (Taming), 44, 45, 81
Ta-t'ung (Tatung), 39, 40, 46, 47, 48
Regional Seminary of, 27, 40, 42, 46-48, 59, 67, 143, 149-151
T'ien-chin (Tientsin), 43, 44
Ting-chou (Tingchow; mod. n. Ch'ang-t'ing), 55
Ts'ao-chou (Tsaochow; mod. n. Ho-tse), 59
T'un-ch'i (Tunki), 51
T'ung-chou (Tungchow; mod. n. Ta-li), 49

Wan-hsien (Wanhsien), 60
Wei-hai-wei (Weihaiwei), 45, 46
Wu-ch'ang (Wuchang), 27, 53
Wu-chou (Wuchow; mod. n. Ts'ang-wu), 58
Wu-hu (Wuhu), 51
Regional Seminary of, 51-52, 59

Yang-ku (Yangku), 59
Yen-an (Yenan), 49
Yen-chou (Yenchow; mod. n. Tzu-yang), 59
Intermissional Seminary of, 52, 59, 69, 81
Yo-chou (Yochow; mod. n. Yüeh-yang), 53
Yüan-ling (Yüanling), 53
Yung-nien (Yungnien), 44, 45, 81
Yung-p'ing (Yungping), 43, 44
Yün-nan (Yünnan), 11, 60
Yü-tz'u (Yütze), 48, 49

## II. Postal Guide Transliteration

Aberdeen (Chinese: Hsiang-kang-tzu), 55
Amoy (Hsia-men), 28, 55
Anhwei (An-hui), 51, 52
Anking (An-ching), 51
Ankwo (An-kuo), 43, 44

Cambodia, 11
Canton (Kuang-chou), 25, 55
Chala (Cha-la), Regional Seminary of, 43-44
Changteh (Ch'ang-te), 53
Chaohsien (Chao-hsien), 43, 44
Chefoo (Chih-fou), 26, 29, 45, 46
Chekiang (Che-chiang), 26, 27, 59, 69, 148
Chengting (Cheng-ting), 43, 44
Chengtu (Ch'eng-tu), 60
Intermissional Seminary of, 60, 69
Chihli (Chih-li), 26, 148
Chowchih (Chou-chih), 49
Chowtsun (Chou-ts'un), 45, 46
Chungking (Ch'ung-ch'ing), 11, 60
Major Seminary of, 60
Cochin-China, 9, 11

Fengsiang (Feng-hsiang), 49
Fenyang (Fen-yang), 43, 82
Foochow (Fu-chou), 55
Fukien (Fu-chien), 28, 54, 56, 79, 81, 155
Regional Seminary of, 54-55 56, 79, 81, 155-156
Funing (Fu-ning), 55

Haimen (Hai-men), 51
Hanchung (Han-chung), 52
Hangchow (Hang-chou), 60
Hankow (Han-k'ou), 53, 122
Regional Seminary of, 52-54, 81, 122
Hingan (Hsing-an), 52
Honan (Ho-nan), 26, 28, 52, 59
Hongkong (Hsiang-kang), 28, 55, 56
Regional Seminary of, 29, 55-58, 79, 154-155
Hopeh (Ho-pei), 43, 45, 81, 82
Hsinking (Hsin-ching), 41, 42
Regional Seminary of, 41-42
Hunan (Hu-nan), 52, 53, 54, 81, 122
Hungkialou (Hung-chia-lou), 45
Hungtung (Hung-tung), 43, 82
Hupeh (Hu-pei), 27, 52, 53, 54, 81, 122

Ichow (I-chou), 59
Iduhsien (I-tu-hsien), 45, 46

Jehol (Je-ho), 39, 40, 42, 48

Kaifeng (K'ai-feng), Regional Seminary of, 52
Kangting (K'ang-ting), 60
Kansu (Kan-su), 49, 50
Kashing (Chia-hsing), 60
Kiangchow (Chiang-chou), 49
Kiangnan (Chiang-nan), 26, 148
Kiangsi (Chiang-hsi), 27
Kiangsu (Chiang-su), 45, 50, 51, 82
Kiating (Chia-ting), 60
Kienow (Chien-ou), 55
Kingchow (Ching-chou), 53
Kinghsien (Ching-hsien), 44, 45, 81
Regional Seminary of, 44-45, 51, 81, 82, 83
Kirin (Chi-lin), 41, 42
Kongmoon (Chiang-men), 55, 57
Kunming (K'un-ming), Major Seminary of, 60
Kwangsi (Kuang-hsi), 58
Kwangtung (Kuang-tung), 55, 56, 58
Kweichow (Kuei-chou), 11
Kweilin (Kuei-lin), 58
Kweisui (Kuei-sui), 48 in note 46

Lanchow (Lan-chou), Regional Seminary of, 49-50
Lichow (Li-chou), 53
Lintsing (Lin-ch'ing), 45, 46
Lishui (Li-shui), 60
Luan (Lu-an), 48, 49

Macau (English: Macao; Chinese: Ao-men), 55, 57, 58
Malacca, 58, 60
Manchuria, 40, 41, 42, 48
Manchoukuo, 41, 42
Mongolia, 26, 40, 48, 148

Nanking (Nan-ching), 51, 52
Ningsia (Ning-hsia), 39, 40, 48
Ningpo (Ning-po), 59, 60
Intermissional Seminary of, 59-60, 69
Ningyüan (Ning-yüan), 60

Pakhoi (Pei-hai), 55, 58
Paoting (Pao-ting), 43, 44
Pehluchang (Pai-lu-ch'ang), 60
Peking (Pei-ching), 43, 44
Penang, General Seminary of, 24, 28, 29, 58, 60
Pengpu (Pang-fou), 51
Pondicherry, Central Seminary of, 10, 11, 24

Sanyüan (San-yüan), 49
Shanghai (Shang-hai), 18, 50, 51
Regional Seminary of, 50-51, 59, 82
Shansi (Shan-hsi), 40, 43, 48, 49, 82
Shantung (Shan-tung), 26, 29, 45, 46, 52, 59, 69, 81, 148

Shaowu (Shao-wu), 55
Shensi (Shen-hsi), 49, 52
Shiuchow (Shao-chou), 55
Shohchow (Shuo-chou), 48, 49
Shunking (Shun-ch'ing), 60
Shunteh (Shun-te), 43, 44
Siam, 9, 10, 11
Sian (Hsi-an), 49
Sienhsien (Hsien-hsien), 44, 45, 81
Sinkiang (Hsin-chiang), 50
Sinsiang (Hsin-hsiang), 52, 59
Sinyang (Hsin-yang), 52, 59
Siwantze (Hsi-wan-tzu), 39, 40, 46, 48
Süancheng (Süan-ch'eng), 51
Süanhwa (Süan-hua), 43
  Regional Seminary of, 42-43, 82
Süchow (Hsü-chou), 45, 51, 82, 83
Suifu (Sui-fu), 60
Suiyüan (Sui-yüan), 39, 40, 48
  Regional Seminary of, 39-40, 42, 48, 59
Swatow (Shan-t'ou), 58
Szechwan (Ssu-ch'uan), 11, 26, 60, 69, 148
  Synod of, 11-13, 14, 17, 100

Taichow (T'ai-chou), 60
Taikiachuang (Tai-chia-chuang), 59
Taiyüan (T'ai-yüan), 48, 49
  Regional Seminary of, 48-49, 82
Taming (Ta-ming), 44, 45, 81
Tatung (Ta-t'ung), 39, 40, 46, 47, 48
  Regional Seminary of, 27, 40, 42, 46-48, 59, 67, 143, 149-151
Tientsin (T'ien-chin), 43, 44
Tingchow (Ting-chou), 55
Tonkin, 8, 9, 11
Tokyo, Regional Seminary of, 90
Tsaochow (Ts'ao-chou), 59
Tsinan (Chi-nan), 45, 46
  Regional Seminary of, 45-46, 69, 81
Tsinchow (Ch'in-chou), 49
Tsinghai (Ch'ing-hai; Mongol: Kokonor), 50
Tsingtao (Ch'ing-tao), 59
Tsining (Chi-ning), 39, 40, 48
Tungchow (T'ung-chou), 49
Tunki (T'un-ch'i), 51

Wanhsien (Wan-hsien), 60
Weihaiwei (Wei-hai-wei), 45, 46
Wuchang (Wu-ch'ang), 27, 53
Wuchow (Wu-chou), 58
Wuhu (Wu-hu), 51
  Regional Seminary of, 51-52, 59

Yangku (Yang-ku), 59
Yenan (Yen-an), 49
Yenchow (Yen-chou), 59
  Intermissional Seminary of, 52, 59, 69, 81
Yihsien (I-hsien), 43
Yochow (Yo-chou), 53
Yüanling (Yüan-ling), 53
Yungnien (Yung-nien), 44, 45, 81
Yungping (Yung-p'ing), 43, 44
Yünnan (Yün-nan), 11, 60
Yütze (Yü-tz'u), 48, 49

Zi-ka-wei (Hsü-chia-hui), 18, 50, 51

## ALPHABETICAL INDEX

Admission to regional seminary, 121-123
Agreement, economic,
  approval of, 108-109
  contents of, 106-108
  for Regional Seminary of Fu-chien, 155- 156
  for Regional Seminary of Hsiang-kang, 55-56, 154-155
Alexander VII, pope, 9

Annual report, 129
Appointment,
of confessors, 94-95
of officials, 92-94
of professors, 92-94, 96-97
of rector, 92-93
Attendance at regional seminary, 80ff.
Augustinian Fathers, 41, 42

Benedict XIV, pope, 9
Benedict XV, pope, 24, 25
Bishop,
proper, for ordination, 116 ff.
proper, for ordination of religious, 120-121
Borromeo, St. Charles,
and the constitution of seminaries, 4
legislation on seminaries, 5
the "Institutiones", 5-6

Clement IX, pope, 9
Clement X, pope, 9
Clement XI, pope, 9
Clement XII, pope, 9
Clement XIII, pope, 10
Clement XIV, pope, 10
Confessors in regional seminary, 94-95
Constitution,
of intermissional seminary, 63 ff.
of regional seminary, 63 ff., 71 ff.
Council,
of China, 18, 31, 32, 88, 99, 103
of Trent, 1-3, 8, 22
Courses,
distribution of, 102
in philosophy, 101-102
in theology, 102
length of, 105

Discipline, rules of, 97 ff.
Dismissal from regional seminary, 123-124
Documents before ordination, 113-114
Domicile,
for ordination, 116 ff.
of students in regional seminary, 118 ff.

Economic agreement, 106-109
Entrance,
into regional seminary, 121-123
into religion forbidden, 10, 84 ff., 90
Examinations, 103
Exemption of regional seminary, 138 ff., 143-146

Franciscans (O.F.M.), 27, 45, 48, 49, 52, 53
Funds, investment of, 108

General Seminary of Siam- Pondicherry-Penang, 10, 11, 24, 28, 29, 58, 60
General Statutes of Central Seminary of Ta-t'ung, 47, 149-151
Guébriant, de,
and the apostolic visitation, 25
his views concerning regional seminaries, 26-27, 148-149
result of his visitation, 27 ff.

*Horarium*, daily, 99

Innocent XI, pope, 9
Institute, religious,
and administration of regional seminary, 92 ff.
and constitution of regional seminary, 77
and economic agreement, 106 ff.
and program of studies, 97 ff., 100-101
and rules of discipline, 97 ff.
Intermissional seminary,
constitution of, 63 ff.

of Ch'eng-tu, 60, 69
of Ning-po, 59-60, 69
of Yen-chou, 52, 59, 69, 81

Jurisdiction,
of local Ordinary over regional seminary, 143-146
of Ordinaries of region over regional seminary, 125, 130-131, 143 ff.

Lazarists (C.M.), 27, 43, 44, 59
Local Ordinary, jurisdiction of, 143 ff.

Meeting of the Ordinaries of the region,
presiding officer, 127-128
secretary, 128-129
subject matter of, 126-127
time of, 127
Milan Foreign Mission Society, 28, 52

Native clergy, 8, 9, 13, 24, 25
*Normae* (1934), text of, 35-39, 74-76, 92, 110-111, 134
*Norme* (1921),
commentary on, 89-91, 131- 133, 146-147
text of, 32-34, 151-153

Oath,
"Alexandrian", 85
for title "of the mission", 86 ff.
Officials, appointment of, 92-94
Ordinaries of region,
and administration of seminary, 124 ff.
and admission of students, 121-123
and annual meeting, 126 ff.
and annual report, 129
and dismissal of students, 123-124
and economic agreement, 106 ff.
and ordination of students, 113 ff.
duties in regard to regional seminary, 125
jurisdiction over regional seminary, 125, 130-131, 143 ff.
Ordinary, local, jurisdiction of, 143-146
Ordination,
documents necessary for, 113-114
domicile necessary for, 116 ff.
investigations before, 115 ff.
of religious, 120-121
of seculars, 113 ff.
Ownership of regional seminary,
in civil law, 79-80
in ecclesiastical law, 77-79

Paris Foreign Mission Society, 11, 24, 28, 29, 60
Philosophy,
course in, 101-102
length of, 105
Pius VI, pope, 11
Pius XI, pope, 24
Preachers, Order of, 54, 155-156
Prefect Apostolic, ordination of students, 120
Professors, appointment of, 92-94, 96-97
Program of studies, 100 ff.

*Ratio studiorum*, 100 ff.
Rector of regional seminary,
and annual meeting, 129-130
and annual report, 129
and appointment of confessors, 95
and dismissal of students, 123-124
appointment of, 92-93
duties of, 113-114, 134 ff., 137 ff.
ordinary power of, 141-143
parochial rights of, 10-11, 138 ff.

rights of, 134 ff., 137 ff.
Region served by regional seminary, 81-83
Regional seminary,
admission to, 121-123
attendance at, 80-83
commitment of, to a religious institute, 77
confessors in, 94-95
constitution of, 22-23, 63-68, 71-73
definition of, 30-31
dismissal from, 123-124
exemption of, 138 ff., 143-146
officials of, 92-94
ownership of, 77-80
professors of, 92-94, 96-97
supreme direction of, 76-79
Regional Seminary,
of Cha-la, 43-44
of Chi-nan (Tsinan), 45-46, 69, 81
of Ching-hsien (Kinghsien), 44-45, 51, 81, 82, 83
of Fu-chien (Fukien), 54-55, 56, 79, 81, 155-156
of Han-k'ou (Hankow), 52-54, 81, 122
of Hsiang-kang (Hongkong), 29, 55-58, 79, 154-155
of Hsin-ching (Hsinking), 41-42
of K'ai-feng, 52
of Lan-chou, 49-50
of Shang-hai, 50-51, 59, 82
of Süan-hua, 42-43, 82
of Sui-yüan, 39-40, 42, 48, 59
of T'ai-yüan, 48-49, 82
of Ta-t'ung, 27, 40, 42, 46-48, 59, 67, 143, 149-151
of Wu-hu, 51-52, 59
Religion, entrance into forbidden, 10, 84 ff., 90
Religious, ordination of, 120-121
Report, annual, 129
Rules of discipline, 97 ff.

Sacred Congregation of *Propaganda*,
and administration of seminary, 76-79
and appointment of officials and professors, 93
and appointment of rector, 72, 93
and constitution of regional seminary, 71-73, 77
and economic agreement, 108-109
and program of studies, 97
and rules of discipline, 97
Scheut Fathers, 40, 46, 47, 143, 149-151
Seminary,
diocesan, 61-62
interdiocesan, 62
intermissional, 68, 70
regional, 62
Society of the Divine Word, 50, 59
Society of Jesus, 44, 50, 51, 52, 55
Spiritual director, 95-96
Studies,
length of, 105
program of, 100 ff.
Superior General,
and administration of regional seminary, 92 ff.
and appointment of officials and professors, 92-93, 96
and appointment of rector, 72, 92-93
and constitution of regional seminary, 77
and economic agreement, 106 ff.
and program of studies, 97 ff., 100-101
and rules of discipline, 97
Synod of Ssu-ch'uan (Szechwan), 11, 12-13, 14, 17, 100

Textbooks, 104
Theology,
  course in, 102
  length of, 105
Thomas, St., 104
Title "of the mission", 85-89
Vacations, 99-100
Visitation,
  apostolic, 25-27
  canonical, 145

## BIOGRAPHICAL NOTE

MARCIAN JOHN MATHIS was born in Chicago, Illinois, on March 23, 1918. He attended the parochial school of St. Augustine in Chicago. In June of 1937 he graduated from St. Joseph College, Westmont, Illinois, entered the novitiate of the Franciscan Order at Teutopolis, Illinois, and in the following year made his religious profession as a member of the Order of Friars Minor. After completing his philosophical studies in Our Lady of Angels Seminary, Cleveland, Ohio, and his theological studies at St. Joseph Seminary, Teutopolis, Illinois, he was ordained to the priesthood on June 22, 1944. In February, 1946, he enrolled in the School of Canon Law of the Catholic University of America, where he received the degree of the Baccalaureate in Canon Law in February of 1947, and the degree of the Licentiate in Canon Law in February of 1948.

## MAP OF CHINA SHOWING LOCATIO

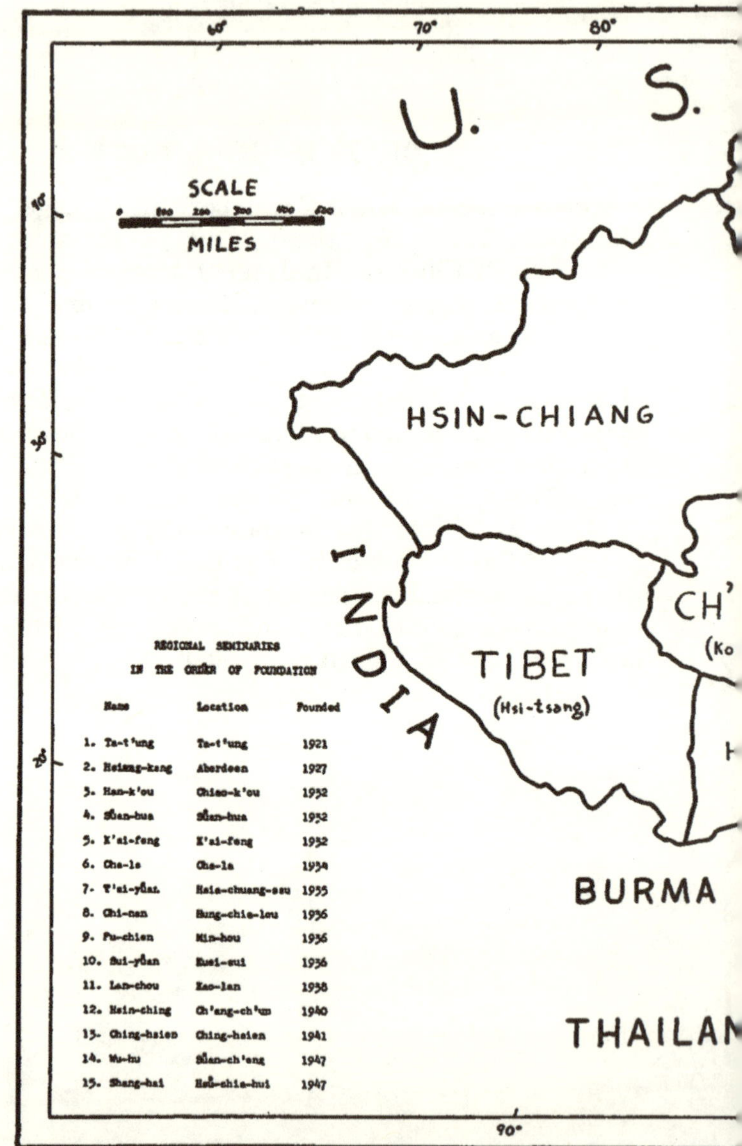


REGIONAL SEMINARIES
IN THE ORDER OF FOUNDATION

| Name | Location | Founded |
|---|---|---|
| 1. Ta-t'ung | Ta-t'ung | 1921 |
| 2. Hsiang-kang | Aberdeen | 1927 |
| 3. Han-k'ou | Chiao-k'ou | 1932 |
| 4. Süan-hua | Süan-hua | 1932 |
| 5. K'ai-feng | K'ai-feng | 1932 |
| 6. Cha-la | Cha-la | 1934 |
| 7. T'ai-yüan | Hsia-chuang-ssu | 1935 |
| 8. Chi-nan | Hung-chia-lou | 1936 |
| 9. Fu-chien | Min-hou | 1936 |
| 10. Sui-yüan | Kuei-sui | 1936 |
| 11. Lan-chou | Kao-lan | 1938 |
| 12. Hsin-ching | Ch'ang-ch'un | 1940 |
| 13. Ching-hsien | Ching-hsien | 1941 |
| 14. Wu-hu | Süan-ch'eng | 1947 |
| 15. Shang-hai | Hsü-chia-hui | 1947 |

## OF THE REGIONAL SEMINARIES

## CANON LAW STUDIES*

327. Koesler, Rev. Leo J., O.S.B., J.C.L., Entrance into the Novitiate by Clerics in Major Orders (Canon 542, 2°).
328. McFarland, Rev. Norman E., J.C.L., Essential Conditions and Sufficient Signs of Vocation to the Religious Life.
329. Wiest, Rev. Donald Herman, O.F.M. Cap., S.T.B., J.C.L., The Precensorship of Books.
330. De Witt, Rev. Max George, A.B., J.C.L., The Cessation of Delegated Power.
331. Mathis, Rev. Marcian John, O.F.M., J.C.L., The Constitution and Supreme Administration of Regional Seminaries Subject to the Sacred Congregation for the Propagation of the Faith in China.
332. Schorr, Rev. George F., A.B., J.C.L., The Law of the Celebret.
333. Sheehy, Rev. Robert Francis, A.B., J.C.L., The Sacred Congregation of the Sacraments: Its Competence in the Roman Curia.
334. Shields, Rev. Joseph A., A.B., J.C.L., Deprivation of the Clerical Garb.
335. Uricheck, Rev. George Edward, A.B., J.C.L., De forma celebrationis matrimonii in Ecclesiis Orientalibus ante Motu Proprio *Crebrae Allatae* et post.
336. De Pauw, Rev. Gommar Albert Leo Julian Maria, J.C.L., The Legal Status of Catholic Elementary Schools in Belgium, 1830-1950.

---

* For a complete list of the available numbers of this series apply to the Catholic University of America Press, 620 Michigan Avenue, N. E., Washington 17, D. C.